OUTLOOK

for Beginners
Step-by-Step Instructions

Kiet Huynh

Table of Contents

CHAPTER I
Introduction to Outlook

1.1 What is Outlook?

 Microsoft Outlook is a comprehensive personal information manager that is widely used across the globe for handling emails, managing calendars, organizing contacts, and much more. Originally launched in 1997, Outlook has evolved significantly over the years, becoming an essential tool for both personal and professional communication and organization.

History and Evolution of Outlook

Outlook's history dates back to its initial release as part of Microsoft Office 97. Over the years, it has undergone numerous updates and enhancements, incorporating feedback from millions of users worldwide. Each new version of Outlook has brought more features and improvements, making it a robust and versatile tool for managing information.

The evolution of Outlook can be summarized through its major releases:

- Outlook 97: The first version that introduced basic email and calendar functionalities.

- Outlook 2000 and 2003: These versions added more advanced features like improved HTML email support and better integration with other Office applications.

- Outlook 2007: Introduced the Ribbon interface, making it easier for users to access features and tools.

- Outlook 2010 and 2013: Brought significant improvements in performance, search capabilities, and social connectivity.

- Outlook 2016 and 2019: Focused on enhancing collaboration with features like Groups and improved cloud integration.

- Outlook 365: The latest cloud-based version, providing continuous updates and seamless integration with other Microsoft services.

Core Functions of Outlook

Outlook is designed to be a one-stop solution for managing various types of information. Its core functions include:

- Email Management: At its heart, Outlook is an email client. It allows users to send, receive, and manage emails from multiple accounts. Features like spam filtering, email categorization, and conversation threading help users keep their inboxes organized.

- Calendar Management: Outlook's calendar is a powerful tool for scheduling appointments, meetings, and events. It supports multiple calendars, shared calendars, and the ability to set reminders and alerts.

- Contact Management: Outlook provides a centralized address book where users can store and manage contact information. It supports the creation of contact groups and detailed contact records.

- Task Management: Users can create, assign, and track tasks. This feature is particularly useful for project management and personal productivity.

- Notes and Journals: Outlook includes tools for creating notes and journal entries, allowing users to keep track of important information and daily activities.

Outlook's User Interface

The user interface of Outlook is designed to be intuitive and user-friendly. It consists of several key components:

- Ribbon: A toolbar at the top of the screen that provides access to all of Outlook's features and tools. It is organized into tabs, each containing related commands and options.

- Navigation Pane: Located on the left side of the screen, the navigation pane allows users to switch between Mail, Calendar, People, Tasks, and Notes. It also provides quick access to folders and other frequently used items.

- Reading Pane: This pane displays the content of selected emails, appointments, or tasks. It can be positioned at the bottom or right side of the screen.

- To-Do Bar: An optional pane that displays upcoming appointments, tasks, and flagged emails.

Integration with Other Microsoft Services

One of Outlook's greatest strengths is its integration with other Microsoft services. This integration enhances productivity and makes it easier for users to collaborate and share information.

- Office Suite Integration: Outlook seamlessly integrates with other Microsoft Office applications like Word, Excel, and PowerPoint. Users can easily attach Office documents to emails, share calendars, and import/export data between applications.

- OneDrive: Integration with OneDrive allows users to store and share files in the cloud. Attachments can be saved directly to OneDrive, and links to files can be shared instead of large attachments.

- Teams and Skype: Outlook integrates with Microsoft Teams and Skype, enabling users to schedule and join virtual meetings, chat with colleagues, and make voice or video calls.

- Exchange Server: For business users, Outlook integrates with Microsoft Exchange Server, providing advanced features like shared mailboxes, public folders, and enhanced security and compliance.

Versions of Outlook

Outlook is available in several versions, each catering to different user needs and preferences:

- Outlook Desktop App: Part of the Microsoft Office Suite, the desktop app is a powerful tool for Windows and Mac users. It offers the full range of features and is ideal for users who need advanced functionality.

- Outlook on the Web: Also known as Outlook Web App (OWA), this version allows users to access their Outlook account from any web browser. It is particularly useful for users who need to access their email and calendar on the go.

- Outlook Mobile App: Available for iOS and Android devices, the mobile app provides a streamlined experience for managing emails, calendars, and contacts on smartphones and tablets.

- Outlook 365: A cloud-based version that is part of the Microsoft 365 subscription. It provides continuous updates and additional features like cloud storage, collaboration tools, and AI-powered insights.

Key Features of Outlook

Outlook is packed with features that help users manage their information efficiently. Some of the key features include:

- Focused Inbox: This feature separates important emails from less important ones, helping users focus on what matters most.

- Search: Outlook's powerful search functionality allows users to quickly find emails, attachments, and other information.

- Quick Steps: Users can create custom actions to automate repetitive tasks, such as moving emails to specific folders or forwarding emails to a group.

- Rules and Alerts: Rules can be set up to automate email management, such as moving emails from specific senders to designated folders or setting alerts for important messages.

- Calendar Sharing: Users can share their calendars with colleagues, making it easier to schedule meetings and coordinate activities.

- Mail Merge: Outlook supports mail merge with Word, enabling users to send personalized emails to multiple recipients.

- Integrated Task Management: Tasks can be created from emails, and users can track their progress directly within Outlook.

- Email Templates: Users can create and use templates for common email responses, saving time and ensuring consistency.

- Customizable Views: Outlook allows users to customize their views, such as displaying the calendar alongside the inbox or changing the layout of the reading pane.

Benefits of Using Outlook

Outlook offers numerous benefits that make it a preferred choice for individuals and organizations:

- Productivity: With its comprehensive set of tools, Outlook helps users manage their time and information more effectively. Features like calendar reminders, task management, and email organization contribute to increased productivity.

- Collaboration: Outlook's integration with Microsoft Teams, OneDrive, and other collaboration tools makes it easy for users to work together, share information, and stay connected.

- Flexibility: Whether on a desktop, web browser, or mobile device, Outlook provides a consistent experience, allowing users to access their information from anywhere.

- Security: Outlook offers robust security features, including encryption, two-factor authentication, and advanced threat protection, ensuring that users' information is safe and secure.

- Customization: Users can tailor Outlook to their specific needs by customizing views, creating rules and alerts, and using add-ins to extend functionality.

Conclusion

Microsoft Outlook is more than just an email client; it is a comprehensive personal information manager that helps users stay organized, productive, and connected. Its wide range of features, seamless integration with other Microsoft services, and flexible deployment options make it a valuable tool for both personal and professional use. Understanding what Outlook is and how it has evolved over time provides a solid foundation for beginners to start exploring its capabilities and harnessing its full potential.

1.2 Benefits of Using Outlook

Outlook, part of the Microsoft Office Suite, is a robust email client and personal information manager widely used in both personal and professional settings. Its extensive features and capabilities offer numerous benefits to users, enhancing productivity, organization, and communication. In this section, we will delve into the various benefits of using Outlook, highlighting how it can improve your daily tasks and streamline your workflow.

1.2.1 Comprehensive Email Management

One of the primary benefits of Outlook is its comprehensive email management capabilities. Outlook provides a unified platform where you can manage multiple email accounts, including those from different providers such as Gmail, Yahoo, and Exchange. This allows you to centralize your email communications in one place, reducing the need to switch between different applications.

a. Unified Inbox

The unified inbox feature in Outlook allows users to view and manage emails from multiple accounts in a single inbox. This feature is particularly useful for users with several email addresses, as it streamlines the process of checking and responding to emails. By consolidating emails into one inbox, users can save time and ensure that no important messages are overlooked.

b. Advanced Filtering and Organization

Outlook offers advanced filtering and organization tools that help users keep their inboxes clutter-free. With features like rules, categories, and folders, users can automatically sort incoming emails based on specific criteria, such as sender, subject, or keywords. This helps prioritize important emails and reduces the time spent manually sorting through messages.

c. Conversation View

The conversation view in Outlook groups related emails into threads, making it easier to follow and manage email discussions. This feature ensures that all replies and forwards related to an initial email are displayed together, providing a clear overview of the conversation history. It helps users stay organized and quickly locate specific messages within a thread

1.2.2 Enhanced Productivity and Time Management

Outlook is designed to enhance productivity and time management through its integrated calendar, task, and scheduling features. These tools enable users to plan and manage their time effectively, ensuring that they stay on top of their commitments and deadlines.

a. Integrated Calendar

Outlook's integrated calendar is a powerful tool for managing appointments, meetings, and events. Users can create and customize multiple calendars, allowing them to separate personal and professional schedules. The calendar also supports shared calendars, enabling team members to view each other's availability and schedule meetings more efficiently.

b. Meeting Scheduling

The meeting scheduling feature in Outlook simplifies the process of organizing meetings. Users can send meeting requests, check attendees' availability, and reserve meeting rooms directly from their Outlook calendar. The scheduling assistant helps find suitable meeting times by displaying the availability of all participants, minimizing scheduling conflicts and reducing the back-and-forth communication typically involved in organizing meetings.

c. Task Management

Outlook's task management capabilities help users keep track of their to-do lists and deadlines. Users can create tasks, set due dates, assign priorities, and categorize tasks for better organization. The task list integrates seamlessly with the calendar, allowing users to view and manage their tasks alongside their appointments and events. This integration ensures that tasks are not overlooked and helps users stay focused on their priorities.

1.2.3 Improved Collaboration and Communication

Outlook's collaboration and communication features are designed to facilitate teamwork and streamline communication within organizations. By providing a unified platform for email, calendar, and contacts, Outlook enhances the way users interact and collaborate with colleagues.

a. Shared Calendars and Contacts

Shared calendars and contacts in Outlook enable teams to collaborate more effectively. Shared calendars allow team members to view each other's schedules, making it easier to coordinate meetings and events. Shared contacts provide a centralized address book that can be accessed by all team members, ensuring that contact information is up-to-date and easily accessible.

b. Email Collaboration

Outlook's email collaboration features, such as shared mailboxes and distribution groups, improve communication within teams. Shared mailboxes allow multiple users to access and manage a common email account, facilitating team-based email management. Distribution groups enable users to send emails to multiple recipients with a single address, streamlining group communication and ensuring that important information is disseminated efficiently.

c. Integration with Microsoft Teams

Outlook's integration with Microsoft Teams enhances collaboration by providing seamless access to Teams features directly from the Outlook interface. Users can schedule Teams meetings, join video calls, and access Teams chat and collaboration tools without leaving Outlook. This integration streamlines communication and ensures that all collaboration tools are easily accessible in one place.

1.2.4 Robust Security and Compliance

Outlook offers robust security and compliance features that protect users' data and ensure that organizations adhere to regulatory requirements. These features are particularly important for businesses and individuals who handle sensitive information.

a. Data Encryption

Outlook supports data encryption to protect the confidentiality of email communications. Users can encrypt their emails to ensure that only the intended recipients can read the message. Encryption is especially important when sending sensitive information, as it prevents unauthorized access and protects the privacy of the communication.

b. Advanced Threat Protection

Outlook includes advanced threat protection features that help safeguard users from phishing attacks, malware, and other security threats. These features analyze email attachments and links for potential threats and provide real-time alerts to users. By proactively identifying and blocking malicious content, Outlook helps protect users' data and reduces the risk of security breaches.

c. Compliance and Data Governance

Outlook's compliance and data governance features help organizations adhere to regulatory requirements and manage their data effectively. Features such as data loss prevention (DLP), retention policies, and eDiscovery ensure that sensitive information is protected and that organizations can manage and retrieve data in compliance with legal and regulatory standards.

1.2.5 Customization and Personalization

Outlook offers a high degree of customization and personalization, allowing users to tailor the application to their specific needs and preferences. This flexibility enhances the user experience and ensures that Outlook meets the unique requirements of each user.

a. Customizable Interface

Users can customize the Outlook interface to suit their preferences. This includes adjusting the layout, choosing color themes, and configuring the ribbon and navigation pane. By personalizing the interface, users can create a more comfortable and efficient working environment.

b. Custom Rules and Alerts

Outlook allows users to create custom rules and alerts to automate email management and stay informed about important messages. Users can set up rules to automatically move, flag, or categorize emails based on specific criteria. Custom alerts notify users about important emails, upcoming events, or task deadlines, ensuring that they stay on top of their priorities.

c. Add-Ins and Integrations

Outlook supports a wide range of add-ins and integrations that extend its functionality and connect it with other applications and services. Users can install add-ins to enhance email productivity, integrate with project management tools, or access third-party services directly from Outlook. These integrations streamline workflows and ensure that users have access to all the tools they need within a single platform.

1.2.6 Cross-Platform Accessibility

Outlook is available across multiple platforms, including Windows, Mac, iOS, and Android, providing users with consistent access to their email, calendar, and contacts regardless of the device they are using. This cross-platform accessibility ensures that users can stay connected and manage their communications from anywhere.

a. Outlook Mobile App

The Outlook mobile app provides a user-friendly interface for managing email, calendar, and contacts on the go. The app includes features such as focused inbox, calendar integration, and customizable swipe gestures, making it easy for users to stay productive on their mobile devices. The app also supports offline access, allowing users to read and compose emails even without an internet connection.

b. Web Access

Outlook Web Access (OWA) allows users to access their Outlook account from any web browser. OWA provides a similar interface to the desktop application, ensuring a seamless experience across different platforms. This feature is particularly useful for users who need to access their email and calendar from public computers or devices that do not have the Outlook application installed.

1.2.7 Seamless Integration with Microsoft Office

Outlook's seamless integration with other Microsoft Office applications, such as Word, Excel, and PowerPoint, enhances productivity and simplifies workflows. This integration allows users to easily share and collaborate on documents, manage email attachments, and access Office features directly from Outlook.

a. Document Collaboration

Outlook's integration with Office applications facilitates document collaboration by allowing users to share and co-author documents directly from their email. Users can send links to OneDrive or SharePoint files, enabling recipients to access and edit the documents in real-time. This streamlines collaboration and ensures that all team members have access to the latest version of the document.

b. Email Attachments

Outlook simplifies the process of managing email attachments by providing options to attach files from OneDrive, SharePoint, or the local device. Users can also preview attachments within the email without downloading them, saving time and reducing the risk of downloading malicious files. The attachment management features ensure that users can easily share and access documents while maintaining security.

c. Access to Office Features

Outlook users can access various Office features directly from the application, such as inserting tables, charts, and graphics into emails, or using Excel formulas and functions within the email body. This integration enhances the functionality of email communication and allows users to leverage the full capabilities of Office applications within Outlook.

Conclusion

Outlook's extensive features and capabilities offer numerous benefits to users, making it an essential tool for managing email, calendar, tasks, and contacts. Its comprehensive email management, enhanced productivity and time management tools, improved collaboration and communication features, robust security and compliance, customization and personalization options, cross-platform accessibility, and seamless integration with Microsoft Office collectively contribute to a superior user experience. Whether you are a personal user or a business professional, Outlook provides the tools you need to stay organized, productive, and connected.

1.3 Overview of Outlook Features

Microsoft Outlook is a robust email and personal information management tool that offers a wide range of features designed to improve productivity and streamline communication. In this section, we will provide an overview of the key features of Outlook, highlighting how each one can be utilized effectively.

1.3.1 Email Management

Outlook's primary function is email management, and it excels in organizing and streamlining your email communication. The key components of email management in Outlook include:

- Inbox Organization: Outlook provides multiple tools to help you organize your inbox. You can sort emails by date, sender, subject, and other criteria. The conversation view groups emails by thread, making it easier to follow discussions.

- Folders: You can create custom folders to organize your emails. For example, you might have folders for work, personal correspondence, projects, and more.

- Categories: Emails can be tagged with color-coded categories, allowing for quick identification and sorting. You can customize these categories to fit your needs.

- Flags and Reminders: You can flag important emails and set reminders to follow up on them. This feature ensures that critical tasks and messages are not overlooked.

- Search Functionality: Outlook's advanced search capabilities allow you to quickly locate specific emails. You can search by keywords, sender, date range, and more.

1.3.2 Calendar

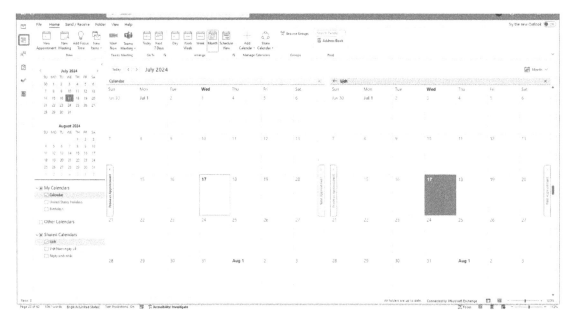

The calendar feature in Outlook is a powerful tool for managing your schedule. Key calendar features include:

- Appointment Scheduling: You can schedule appointments, specifying the date, time, location, and duration. Recurring appointments can be set for regular events.

- Meeting Requests: Outlook allows you to send meeting invitations to others. Attendees can accept or decline invitations, and you can track their responses.

- Calendar Views: You can view your calendar by day, week, or month. The schedule view offers a detailed look at your appointments and meetings.

- Reminders and Alerts: You can set reminders for appointments and meetings, ensuring that you never miss an important event.

- Shared Calendars: You can share your calendar with colleagues, allowing them to view your availability and schedule meetings accordingly.

1.3.3 Contacts

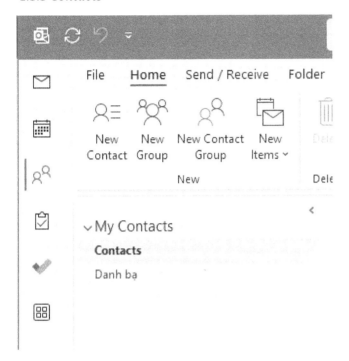

Outlook's contact management features help you keep track of your professional and personal connections. Key features include:

- Contact Creation: You can create detailed contact records, including names, addresses, phone numbers, and email addresses.

- Contact Groups: You can create groups of contacts for easier communication. For example, you might have groups for your team, clients, or family.

- Import and Export: Outlook allows you to import contacts from other applications and export your contact list for backup or sharing.

1.3.4 Tasks and To-Do Lists

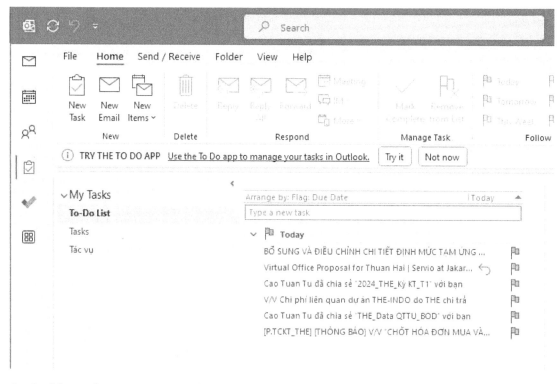

Outlook's task management features help you stay organized and on top of your responsibilities. Key features include:

- Task Creation: You can create tasks, specifying details such as due dates, priority levels, and notes.

- Task Organization: Tasks can be categorized and flagged, making it easier to prioritize and manage your workload.

- To-Do List: The To-Do list consolidates your tasks and flagged emails into a single view, providing an overview of your pending tasks.

1.3.5 Notes and Journal

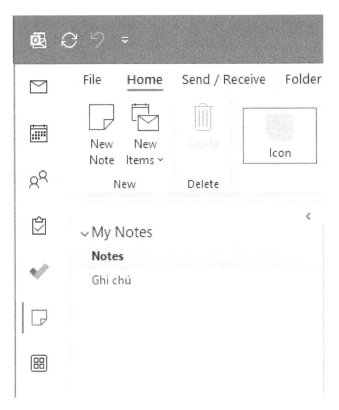

Outlook includes features for keeping notes and tracking activities. Key features include:

- Notes: You can create notes for quick reference. Notes can be color-coded and organized for easy access.

- Journal: The journal feature allows you to track activities and interactions, such as phone calls and meetings. This can be useful for billing or record-keeping purposes.

1.3.6 Email Filtering and Rules

Outlook provides advanced tools for managing your emails through filtering and rules. Key features include:

- Rules: You can create rules to automatically sort incoming emails. For example, you can move emails from specific senders to designated folders.

- Junk Email Filtering: Outlook's junk email filter helps keep your inbox free from spam. You can customize the filter settings to suit your needs.

- Focused Inbox: The Focused Inbox separates important emails from less critical ones, helping you focus on what matters most.

1.3.7 Integration with Other Microsoft Office Applications

Outlook integrates seamlessly with other Microsoft Office applications, enhancing its functionality. Key integrations include:

- Microsoft Word: You can use Word's advanced formatting tools when composing emails in Outlook.

- Microsoft Excel: You can import data from Excel into Outlook, such as contact lists or appointment schedules.

- Microsoft OneNote: You can link emails and calendar events to OneNote, allowing for more detailed note-taking and organization.

1.3.8 Mobile and Web Access

Outlook is accessible on various platforms, ensuring you can stay connected and productive from anywhere. Key access features include:

- Mobile App: Outlook's mobile app provides access to your emails, calendar, and contacts on the go. The app is available for both iOS and Android devices.

- Web Access: Outlook on the web offers a full-featured web interface. You can access your Outlook account from any web browser, ensuring you are not tied to a single device.

1.3.9 Security Features

Outlook includes robust security features to protect your data and privacy. Key features include:

- Encryption: You can encrypt emails to ensure they are only readable by the intended recipient.

- Spam and Phishing Protection: Outlook's filters protect you from spam and phishing attempts.

- Two-Factor Authentication: You can enable two-factor authentication for an added layer of security.

1.3.10 Customization and Personalization

Outlook offers a range of customization options, allowing you to tailor the application to your preferences. Key customization features include:

- Themes and Colors: You can choose from a variety of themes and color schemes to personalize the look of Outlook.

- Quick Access Toolbar: You can customize the Quick Access Toolbar to include the commands you use most frequently.

- Layout Options: You can adjust the layout of the Outlook interface, such as the position of the reading pane and the arrangement of the navigation pane.

Conclusion

Understanding the wide range of features available in Outlook is the first step towards maximizing your productivity and efficiency. Each feature is designed to help you manage your communications and schedule effectively. In the subsequent chapters, we will delve deeper into each of these features, providing detailed instructions and tips for using Outlook to its full potential. By the end of this guide, you will be well-equipped to harness the power of Outlook for your personal and professional needs.

1.4 Setting Up Your Outlook Account

Setting up your Outlook account is the first step towards harnessing its powerful features for email communication, scheduling, and more. This section will guide you through the process of creating and configuring your Outlook account to ensure optimal functionality and efficiency.

Creating Your Outlook Account

To begin using Outlook, you need to create an account that will serve as your gateway to managing emails, calendars, contacts, tasks, and notes seamlessly. Follow these steps to set up your Outlook account:

1. Choosing Your Account Type

Outlook offers different account types, including Microsoft 365, Exchange, Outlook.com, and IMAP/POP accounts. Select the account type that best suits your needs, whether it's for personal use or business purposes.

2. Creating a Microsoft 365 Account

  - Step 1: Navigate to Microsoft 365 Portal

   - Visit the Microsoft 365 portal and select the option to create a new account.

  - Step 2: Account Information

   - Enter your preferred email address and create a strong password. Ensure that your password meets the security requirements specified by Microsoft.

  - Step 3: Verification

   - Verify your identity through a verification code sent to your alternate email address or phone number.

  - Step 4: Account Setup

   - Complete the account setup process by providing additional information such as your name, birthdate, and country/region.

  - Step 5: Agree to Terms

- Review and accept Microsoft's terms of service and privacy policy to proceed.

3. Setting Up an Exchange Account

  - Step 1: Exchange Server Information

  - Obtain the server settings and credentials from your IT administrator or email provider.

  - Step 2: Account Configuration

  - Enter the Exchange server settings including server name, username, and password in Outlook's account setup wizard.

  - Step 3: Account Verification

  - Verify your account settings to ensure connectivity with the Exchange server.

4. Adding an Outlook.com Account

  - Step 1: Sign Up

  - Navigate to Outlook.com and select "Create account" to begin the signup process.

  - Step 2: Account Details

  - Enter your desired email address and create a password. Choose an available domain (e.g., @outlook.com, @hotmail.com).

  - Step 3: Verification

  - Verify your identity using a verification code sent to your phone number or alternate email address.

  - Step 4: Additional Information

  - Provide additional information such as your name, birthdate, and country/region to complete the account setup.

5. Configuring an IMAP/POP Account

  - Step 1: Account Type Selection

  - Choose between IMAP (Internet Message Access Protocol) or POP (Post Office Protocol) based on your email provider's server settings.

  - Step 2: Server Settings

- Enter the incoming and outgoing server settings provided by your email provider, along with your username and password.

- Step 3: Account Verification

- Verify the account settings and test connectivity to ensure proper configuration.

Configuring Outlook Settings

Once your account is created, it's essential to configure Outlook settings to personalize your experience and optimize productivity:

- Personal Information Settings

- Update your profile information including name, title, and contact details.

- Email Settings

- Customize email signature, set default sending options, and manage email encryption settings.

- Calendar Settings

- Adjust calendar display preferences, time zone settings, and default meeting reminders.

- Contact Settings

- Configure contact layout and synchronization options with other devices or accounts.

- Security Settings

- Enhance account security by enabling two-factor authentication (2FA), managing trusted devices, and reviewing recent activity.

Syncing Outlook Across Devices

To ensure seamless access to your Outlook data from multiple devices, consider syncing your account:

- Microsoft 365 Integration

- Utilize Microsoft 365's cloud-based services to automatically sync emails, calendar events, and contacts across devices.

- Device-Specific Settings

- Configure IMAP/POP or Exchange settings on each device (e.g., desktop, mobile) to synchronize Outlook data locally.

Troubleshooting Common Setup Issues

Encountering setup issues is common when configuring Outlook accounts. Here are some troubleshooting tips:

- Check Internet Connectivity

- Ensure stable internet connection to avoid interruptions during account setup or synchronization.

- Verify Account Credentials

- Double-check username, password, and server settings for accuracy and compatibility with Outlook.

- Update Software

- Ensure that Outlook and your operating system are updated to the latest versions to resolve compatibility issues.

Conclusion

Setting up your Outlook account is an essential first step towards leveraging its robust features for enhanced communication and organization. By following these detailed instructions, you can establish your account with confidence, ensuring a seamless experience across all your devices.

This section provides a comprehensive guide to setting up and configuring your Outlook account, empowering you to manage your email, calendar, contacts, and tasks efficiently.

CHAPTER II
Getting Started with Outlook

2.1 Installing Outlook

2.1.1 System Requirements

Before installing Outlook, ensure that your computer meets the following system requirements:

- Operating System: Outlook is compatible with Windows 10, Windows 8.1, and Windows 7 Service Pack 1, as well as macOS versions supported by Microsoft 365.

- Processor: Minimum 1 GHz or faster processor, 32-bit (x86) or 64-bit (x64) processor.

- RAM: Minimum 1 GB RAM for 32-bit; 2 GB for 64-bit.

- Hard Disk Space: Minimum 3 GB available disk space.

- Display: Screen resolution of at least 1280 x 800 pixels.

- Graphics: Graphics hardware acceleration requires DirectX 10 graphics card.

Installation Steps

Follow these steps to install Outlook on your computer:

1. Access Microsoft Office: If you have a Microsoft 365 subscription or purchased Outlook separately, visit the Microsoft Office website or use the Microsoft Store app on your computer to begin the installation process.

2. Sign In: Sign in with your Microsoft account associated with your Office subscription. If you don't have an account, you can create one during the sign-in process.

3. Choose Installation Type: Select "Install Office" and then "Install" to begin downloading the Office installer.

4. Run the Installer: Once the download is complete, run the installer file to start the installation process.

5. Follow Installation Prompts: Follow the on-screen prompts to complete the installation. You may need to agree to the license terms and choose the installation location.

6. Installation Progress: Outlook and other Office apps will be installed. This may take several minutes depending on your internet speed and computer performance.

7. Launch Outlook: Once installation is complete, launch Outlook from the Start menu (Windows) or Applications folder (macOS).

8. Activate Outlook: If prompted, sign in to activate Outlook with your Microsoft account or enter the product key if you purchased Outlook separately.

9. Set Up Your Profile: Follow the setup wizard to configure your Outlook profile, including adding your email account(s) and personalizing settings.

10. Update Office: After installation, it's recommended to check for and install any available updates to ensure you have the latest features and security patches.

Following these steps will ensure you successfully install Outlook on your computer and set it up for use according to your preferences.

2.1.2 Installation Steps

Installing Outlook is a straightforward process that involves a few key steps to ensure proper setup on your computer. Follow these instructions to install Outlook:

1. Prepare Your System:

   Before you begin, ensure that your computer meets the minimum system requirements for installing Outlook. This typically includes:

- Operating System: Outlook is compatible with Windows and macOS. Check Microsoft's official website for specific version compatibility.

- Disk Space: Ensure you have sufficient free space on your hard drive to install the application.

- Internet Connection: A stable internet connection may be required for downloading the installation files and updates.

2. Download Outlook:

- If you haven't already obtained the installation files, visit the Microsoft Office website or use your Office 365 subscription account to download the Outlook installer.

- Sign in with your Microsoft account associated with Office 365 or follow the prompts to purchase and download Outlook.

3. Run the Installer:

- Locate the downloaded installer file (typically named something like "setup.exe" on Windows or a disk image file on macOS).

- Double-click the installer file to launch the installation wizard.

4. Follow Installation Wizard Prompts:

- The installation wizard will guide you through the setup process step-by-step.

- Accept the license agreement and choose the installation options (default settings are usually recommended for most users).

5. Complete Installation:

- Once the installation process begins, Outlook will start installing on your computer.

- Depending on your system and internet speed, this process may take several minutes.

- Once installation is complete, you may be prompted to restart your computer. Follow any additional instructions provided by the installation wizard.

6. Configure Outlook:

  - After installation and restart (if required), launch Outlook.

  - You will be prompted to set up your email account(s) or sign in with your Microsoft account.

  - Follow the on-screen instructions to configure your email accounts and customize Outlook settings according to your preferences.

7. Update Outlook (if necessary):

  - After installation, it's advisable to check for and install any available updates for Outlook to ensure you have the latest features and security patches.

  - Outlook typically checks for updates automatically, but you can also manually check for updates in the application settings.

8. Get Familiar with Outlook:

  - Once installation and setup are complete, take some time to explore the Outlook interface.

  - Familiarize yourself with the Ribbon, Navigation Pane, and Reading Pane as described in section 2.3.

Following these steps will help you successfully install Outlook on your computer and prepare it for use in managing your email, calendars, contacts, and tasks effectively.

2.2 Creating an Outlook Account

2.2.1 Personal Account

Creating a personal Outlook account is straightforward and allows you to manage your emails, contacts, and calendar seamlessly. Follow these steps to set up your personal Outlook account:

1. Navigate to Outlook Website:

   - Open your web browser and go to the Outlook sign-up page (www.outlook.com).

2. Click on "Create Account":

   - Look for the option to create a new account. Click on "Create account" or "Sign up" to begin.

3. Enter Your Information:

   - Fill out the required fields, including your name, desired email address, and password. Ensure your password is strong and includes a mix of letters, numbers, and special characters for security.

4. Verify Your Account:

   - After entering your information, Outlook may ask you to verify your identity. This could be through a phone number or an alternative email address.

5. Complete the CAPTCHA:

   - To prevent automated account creation, you may need to solve a CAPTCHA puzzle.

6. Agree to Terms and Conditions:

   - Review and agree to Microsoft's terms of service and privacy policy.

7. Set Up Your Profile:

   - Optionally, you can add a profile picture and provide additional information about yourself.

8. Finish and Access Your Account:

   - Once your account is created, you can access Outlook by logging in with your new email address and password.

 Benefits of a Personal Outlook Account:

- Integrated Services: Access not only email but also calendar, contacts, and tasks all from one place.

- Cloud Storage: Store and share files using OneDrive, Microsoft's cloud storage service, directly from Outlook.

- Security: Benefit from Microsoft's robust security features, including spam filtering and encryption, to keep your information safe.

By creating a personal Outlook account, you gain access to a powerful suite of tools that can enhance your productivity and communication efficiency.

2.2.2 Business Account

In Outlook, a Business Account allows you to integrate your email with other Microsoft services such as SharePoint and Teams, providing a unified communication platform within your organization.

Setting Up a Business Account:

Setting up a Business Account in Outlook involves the following steps:

1. Navigate to Office 365 Portal:

  - Visit the Office 365 portal using your web browser.

  - Log in with your business credentials provided by your organization's administrator.

2. Access Outlook:

  - Once logged in, navigate to the Outlook app within the Office 365 portal.

3. Setup Process:

  - Follow the prompts to set up your business email account.

  - Enter your business email address and choose a password as per your organization's password policy.

4. Account Configuration:

  - Configure additional settings such as language preferences and email signature.

5. Integration with Microsoft Services:

  - Utilize the integration options with other Microsoft services like SharePoint and Teams.

  - Ensure that your business account is synchronized with the organization's Active Directory for seamless access to resources.

Benefits of a Business Account:

- Enhanced Security: Business accounts often come with additional security features such as multi-factor authentication (MFA) and data encryption.

- Collaboration Tools: Access to SharePoint for document management and Teams for team collaboration.

- Scalability: Easily scale your email services as your business grows, with the ability to add or remove user accounts as needed.

- Support: Dedicated support from your organization's IT department or Microsoft support for any technical issues.

Managing Your Business Account:

- Password Management: Regularly update your password and adhere to password policies set by your organization.

- Email Configuration: Customize your email settings through the Outlook web app or desktop client to suit your workflow.

- Backup and Recovery: Understand backup and recovery options available for your business emails and data.

By setting up a Business Account in Outlook, you ensure efficient communication and collaboration within your organization while leveraging the robust features of Microsoft's suite of services. This integration enhances productivity and streamlines business operations through centralized communication channels.

2.3 Navigating the Outlook Interface

Understanding the Outlook interface is crucial for maximizing your productivity and efficiency. The interface is designed to provide quick access to all the features you need to manage your email, calendar, contacts, tasks, and more. This section will guide you through the main components of the Outlook interface, starting with the Ribbon.

2.3.1 Ribbon

The Ribbon is one of the most prominent features of the Outlook interface, located at the top of the window. It organizes commands and tools into a series of tabs, each containing related groups of features. The Ribbon is dynamic, meaning it changes based on the task you're performing, ensuring that the most relevant tools are always within reach.

Components of the Ribbon

1. Tabs: The Ribbon is divided into several tabs. Each tab corresponds to a set of related commands and tools. The most commonly used tabs in Outlook include:

  - Home: This is the default tab that appears when you open Outlook. It contains essential commands for managing your emails, such as New Email, Reply, Forward, Delete, and more.

  - Send/Receive: This tab includes commands related to sending and receiving emails, such as Send/Receive All Folders, Work Offline, and Download Address Book.

  - Folder: This tab provides tools for managing your folders, such as creating new folders, renaming, deleting, and managing folder properties.

- View: The View tab allows you to customize the appearance of your Outlook interface, including the layout, reading pane, and window settings.

- File: This tab opens the Backstage view, where you can access options for account settings, print, save, and other file-related tasks.

2. Groups: Each tab is further divided into groups that organize related commands together. For example, in the Home tab, you will find groups like New, Delete, Respond, Quick Steps, Move, and Tags. These groups help you quickly locate the commands you need.

3. Commands: Within each group, you will find individual commands represented by buttons, menus, or drop-down lists. Commands are the actual tools you use to perform actions in Outlook, such as creating a new email, deleting a message, or scheduling a meeting.

Using the Ribbon

1. Navigating Tabs: To switch between tabs, simply click on the tab name. For example, clicking on the Home tab will display all the commands related to managing your emails. Clicking on the Calendar tab will switch the view to your calendar and display relevant commands.

2. Executing Commands: To execute a command, click on the corresponding button in the Ribbon. For example, to create a new email, click the New Email button in the Home tab. Some commands have drop-down arrows that provide additional options or settings. Click the arrow to view and select from the available options.

3. Contextual Tabs: Outlook also features contextual tabs that appear only when needed. For example, when you are working on an email, you might see the Message tab with commands specific to email composition. When you click on a calendar event, you might see the Event tab with tools for managing events.

4. Minimizing the Ribbon: If you prefer a cleaner interface with more workspace, you can minimize the Ribbon. To do this, click the small arrow at the top-right corner of the Ribbon or press `Ctrl + F1`. This will collapse the Ribbon to show only the tab names. You can still access the commands by clicking on the tabs, which will temporarily expand the Ribbon.

Customizing the Ribbon

Outlook allows you to customize the Ribbon to suit your workflow. You can add, remove, or rearrange the tabs and commands to fit your preferences.

1. Customizing Tabs and Groups: To customize the Ribbon, right-click anywhere on the Ribbon and select "Customize the Ribbon." This opens the Customize Ribbon dialog box, where you can modify the existing tabs and groups.

   - Add New Tabs and Groups: Click the "New Tab" or "New Group" button to create a new tab or group. You can then add commands to your new tab or group from the list on the left.

   - Reorder Tabs and Groups: Use the up and down arrows to move tabs and groups into your preferred order.

   - Remove Tabs and Groups: Select the tab or group you want to remove and click the "Remove" button.

2. Adding Commands: To add commands to a tab or group, select the desired tab or group in the Customize Ribbon dialog box. Then, choose the commands from the list on the left and click "Add." You can add any command available in Outlook to your custom tabs and groups.

3. Resetting the Ribbon: If you want to revert to the default Ribbon settings, click the "Reset" button in the Customize Ribbon dialog box and choose either "Reset only selected Ribbon tab" or "Reset all customizations."

 Tips for Using the Ribbon Efficiently

- Keyboard Shortcuts: Many commands in the Ribbon have keyboard shortcuts, which can significantly speed up your workflow. For example, press `Ctrl + N` to create a new email or `Ctrl + R` to reply to a selected email.

- Quick Access Toolbar: For frequently used commands, consider adding them to the Quick Access Toolbar, which is located above the Ribbon. Right-click on a command in the Ribbon and select "Add to Quick Access Toolbar."

- Explore Contextual Tabs: Pay attention to contextual tabs that appear based on the task you're performing. These tabs provide additional tools and commands that can be very helpful for specific tasks.

2.3.2 Navigation Pane

The Navigation Pane is a crucial component of the Outlook interface, serving as the central hub for accessing the various modules and features within Outlook. It provides quick and easy access to your emails, calendar, contacts, tasks, and more. Mastering the Navigation Pane will significantly enhance your productivity and efficiency when using Outlook. This section will cover everything you need to know about the Navigation Pane, including its layout, functionality, and customization options.

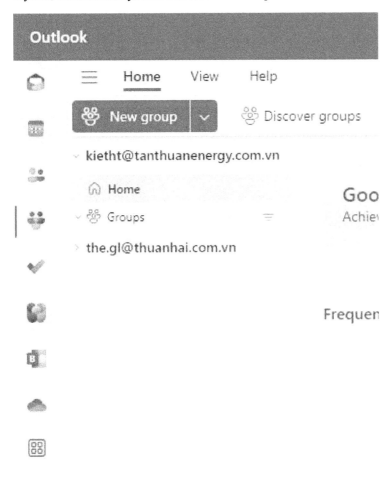

1. Overview of the Navigation Pane

The Navigation Pane is typically located on the left side of the Outlook window. It contains shortcuts to different Outlook modules, such as Mail, Calendar, People, and Tasks. Each module is represented by an icon, and clicking on an icon switches the main window to display the selected module's content.

2. Default Modules in the Navigation Pane

Outlook comes with several default modules accessible via the Navigation Pane:

- Mail: This is the primary module for managing your email messages. It includes your inbox, sent items, drafts, and any other email folders you have created.

- Calendar: The Calendar module allows you to schedule and manage appointments, meetings, and events.

- People (Contacts): This module is used for managing your contact information, including creating, editing, and organizing contact entries.

- Tasks: The Tasks module helps you manage your to-do lists and tasks, allowing you to create, edit, and track tasks.

- Notes: If you use Outlook for taking notes, this module provides access to all your notes.

- Folders: This section provides an overview of all your email folders, allowing you to quickly navigate between them.

3. Customizing the Navigation Pane

Outlook allows you to customize the Navigation Pane to suit your workflow and preferences. Customizations can include rearranging the order of the modules, adding new shortcuts, and adjusting the display settings.

3.1 Rearranging Modules

You can rearrange the order of the modules in the Navigation Pane to prioritize the ones you use most frequently. To do this, simply click and drag the module icons to your desired position.

3.2 Adding and Removing Shortcuts

If there are additional folders or features you frequently access, you can add them as shortcuts to the Navigation Pane:

- Adding Shortcuts: Right-click on the Navigation Pane and select "Navigation Options." In the window that appears, you can add or remove shortcuts by selecting or deselecting the corresponding checkboxes. You can also adjust the number of visible items in the Navigation Pane here.

- Removing Shortcuts: To remove a shortcut, right-click on the shortcut you wish to remove and select "Remove from Favorites."

3.3 Compact Navigation

Outlook offers a "Compact Navigation" option to save space in the Navigation Pane. When enabled, this option reduces the size of the module icons, displaying them as a single row of icons at the bottom of the Navigation Pane. To enable Compact Navigation, right-click on the Navigation Pane and select "Compact Navigation."

4. Using the Mail Module in the Navigation Pane

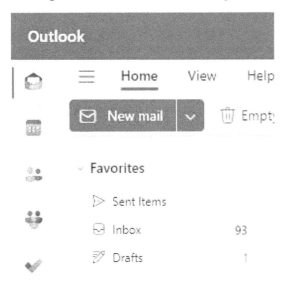

The Mail module is one of the most frequently used sections of the Navigation Pane. It contains various folders that help organize your emails, such as:

- Inbox: Your primary email folder where new messages arrive.

- Sent Items: A folder containing copies of the emails you have sent.

- Drafts: A folder for emails you have started composing but have not yet sent.

- Deleted Items: A folder containing emails you have deleted.

- Junk Email: A folder for spam and potentially harmful emails.

You can also create custom folders within the Mail module to further organize your emails. To create a new folder, right-click on the "Inbox" or any other existing folder, and select "New Folder." Name the folder and press Enter.

5. Using the Calendar Module in the Navigation Pane

The Calendar module helps you manage your schedule by providing a visual representation of your appointments and meetings. The Navigation Pane in the Calendar module includes:

- Calendar Views: Different views such as Day, Work Week, Week, and Month. You can switch between these views to find the one that best suits your needs.

- Calendars: A list of your calendars. You can have multiple calendars for different purposes, such as personal, work, or shared calendars. You can also overlay multiple calendars to see combined schedules.

- Shared Calendars: Calendars shared with you by other people. These can include team calendars, project calendars, or any other shared schedules.

To add a new calendar, right-click on "My Calendars" and select "Add Calendar," then choose whether you want to create a new blank calendar, open a shared calendar, or subscribe to an internet calendar.

6. Using the People (Contacts) Module in the Navigation Pane

The People module, often referred to as Contacts, helps you store and manage information about the people you communicate with. The Navigation Pane in the People module includes:

- Contacts: A list of your saved contacts. You can view your contacts in various views such as People, Business Card, and List.

- Contact Groups: Groups of contacts that you can create to easily send emails to multiple people at once. To create a new group, click on "New Contact Group" in the Ribbon, then add members to the group.

- Address Books: Different address books you have access to, including your personal contacts and any shared address books.

To create a new contact, click on "New Contact" in the Ribbon, fill in the contact details, and save.

7. Using the Tasks Module in the Navigation Pane

The Tasks module helps you track and manage your to-do items. The Navigation Pane in the Tasks module includes:

- My Tasks: A list of your tasks, which can be organized into different task folders.

- To-Do List: A consolidated list of tasks and flagged items from your emails.

- Task Views: Different ways to view your tasks, such as by due date, priority, or status.

To create a new task, click on "New Task" in the Ribbon, enter the task details, and save.

8. Additional Navigation Pane Features

Apart from the main modules, the Navigation Pane offers additional features and options to enhance your productivity:

- Search: A search bar at the top of the Navigation Pane allows you to quickly find emails, contacts, calendar events, and tasks. Simply type your search query and press Enter.

- Favorites: A section at the top of the Navigation Pane where you can add frequently accessed folders or items for quick access. To add an item to Favorites, right-click on it and select "Add to Favorites."

- Shortcuts: You can create shortcuts to other Outlook features or external applications for quick access. To add a shortcut, right-click on the Navigation Pane, select "Shortcuts," and then choose "New Shortcut."

9. Best Practices for Using the Navigation Pane

To make the most of the Navigation Pane, consider the following best practices:

- Keep It Organized: Regularly review and organize your folders and shortcuts to ensure quick and easy access to your most important items.

- Use Favorites: Add frequently used folders to the Favorites section to minimize navigation time.

- Customize to Your Needs: Tailor the Navigation Pane to fit your workflow by adding or removing shortcuts, rearranging modules, and enabling Compact Navigation if needed.

- Leverage Search: Utilize the search feature to quickly find specific items, reducing the time spent manually browsing through folders.

By understanding and effectively utilizing the Navigation Pane, you can significantly enhance your efficiency and productivity in Outlook. This central hub provides quick access to all the essential modules and features you need to manage your emails, schedule, contacts, tasks, and more.

2.3.3 Reading Pane

Outlook's interface is designed to be user-friendly and efficient, allowing you to manage your emails, calendar, contacts, tasks, and notes seamlessly. The key components of the interface include the Ribbon, the Navigation Pane, and the Reading Pane. In this section, we will delve deeper into the Reading Pane, which is essential for viewing and managing your emails.

2.3.3 Reading Pane

The Reading Pane in Outlook is a crucial feature that allows you to preview and read the contents of an email without opening it in a separate window. This functionality enhances productivity by providing a quick glance at the email's content, enabling you to decide whether it requires immediate attention or can be addressed later.

Understanding the Reading Pane

The Reading Pane is typically located to the right or below your list of emails, depending on your layout preference. It displays the full content of the selected email, including the header information (such as the sender, recipient, and subject), the body of the email, and any attachments.

Customizing the Reading Pane

Outlook offers several customization options for the Reading Pane to enhance your reading experience. These options can be accessed through the View tab on the Ribbon:

1. Positioning the Reading Pane:

- Right: This is the default setting, where the Reading Pane is placed to the right of your email list. This layout allows for a wider view of your email content while keeping the list of emails visible.

- Bottom: This setting places the Reading Pane below your email list, which might be preferable if you have a larger monitor or if you want to see more emails in your list.

- Off: You can turn off the Reading Pane entirely, which requires you to double-click on an email to open it in a new window. This option is less common but can be useful if you prefer a minimalist view.

2. Reading Pane Options:

- Mark items as read when viewed in the Reading Pane: This option automatically marks emails as read after you view them in the Reading Pane for a specified period (e.g., 5 seconds). This can help you keep track of which emails you've already reviewed.

- Single key reading using space bar: This feature allows you to scroll through emails using the space bar, making it easier to read lengthy emails without using the mouse.

Using the Reading Pane Effectively

1. Previewing Emails:

The Reading Pane provides a quick way to preview emails without fully opening them. This is particularly useful for quickly scanning through messages to identify important emails that require immediate attention.

2. Managing Attachments:

Attachments in an email are displayed at the top of the Reading Pane. You can open, save, or preview attachments directly from the Reading Pane, making it convenient to access important documents without navigating away from your inbox.

3. Responding to Emails:

You can reply to or forward emails directly from the Reading Pane. Simply click the "Reply," "Reply All," or "Forward" buttons located at the top of the email in the Reading Pane. This functionality streamlines your workflow by allowing you to respond to emails without opening them in a new window.

4. Reading Pane Tips:

- Adjust the size: You can adjust the size of the Reading Pane by clicking and dragging the divider between the Reading Pane and the email list. This allows you to allocate more or less space to the Reading Pane based on your preference.

- Inline replies: When you click "Reply" or "Reply All" while viewing an email in the Reading Pane, Outlook allows you to type your response directly within the Reading Pane. This feature is known as inline replies and helps you respond to emails quickly and efficiently.

Reading Pane in Different Views

1. Compact View:

In Compact View, the Reading Pane is narrower, making it suitable for smaller screens or when you want to see more of your email list. This view is particularly useful when working on laptops or tablets.

2. Expanded View:

In Expanded View, the Reading Pane is wider, providing a more spacious area for reading emails. This view is ideal for desktop monitors or when you need a clearer view of email content, such as when reading long emails or viewing complex email layouts.

Accessibility Features

Outlook's Reading Pane includes several accessibility features to assist users with disabilities:

1. Screen Reader Support:

The Reading Pane is compatible with screen readers, which read the content of the email aloud for visually impaired users. This feature ensures that all users can access and understand their emails.

2. High Contrast Mode:

Outlook supports high contrast mode, which adjusts the colors and contrasts of the interface to make it easier for users with visual impairments to read emails. You can enable this mode through your operating system's accessibility settings.

3. Keyboard Shortcuts:

Outlook provides a range of keyboard shortcuts to navigate and manage emails within the Reading Pane. For example, pressing the arrow keys allows you to move between emails, and pressing "Ctrl + R" lets you reply to an email directly from the Reading Pane.

Troubleshooting Common Issues

1. Reading Pane Not Displaying Properly:

If the Reading Pane is not displaying emails correctly, try the following steps:

- Restart Outlook: Sometimes, simply restarting Outlook can resolve display issues.

- Check View Settings: Ensure that the Reading Pane is enabled in the View tab.

- Update Outlook: Make sure you have the latest updates installed, as updates often fix bugs and improve performance.

2. Emails Not Marking as Read:

If emails are not being marked as read after viewing them in the Reading Pane:

- Check Settings: Go to the View tab, click on "Reading Pane," and ensure that "Mark items as read when viewed in the Reading Pane" is selected.

- Adjust Timing: If the timing is too short, you may not be viewing the email long enough for it to be marked as read. Adjust the timing to a longer duration in the Reading Pane options.

3. Attachments Not Opening:

If attachments are not opening from the Reading Pane:

- Check Security Settings: Some attachments may be blocked for security reasons. Check your security settings to see if they need adjustment.

- Save and Open: Try saving the attachment to your computer and opening it from there.

Conclusion

The Reading Pane in Outlook is an essential tool for efficiently managing your emails. By understanding how to customize and use the Reading Pane effectively, you can streamline your email workflow, quickly preview and respond to messages, and keep your inbox organized. Whether you are dealing with a high volume of emails daily or just a few important messages, mastering the Reading Pane will significantly enhance your Outlook experience.

CHAPTER III
Managing Emails

3.1 Composing and Sending Emails

Email communication is one of the most fundamental features of Microsoft Outlook, and mastering it is crucial for efficient communication. This section will guide you through the essential steps of composing and sending emails, ensuring you make the most of Outlook's capabilities.

3.1.1 Creating a New Email

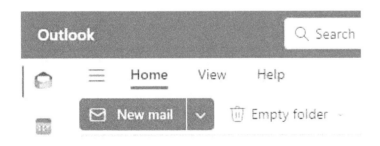

Creating a new email in Outlook is straightforward and intuitive, but there are numerous features and options available to enhance your email creation process. In this subsection, we will cover everything from the basic steps to more advanced techniques to ensure your emails are professional, clear, and effective.

Step-by-Step Guide to Creating a New Email:

1. Opening the New Email Window:

- To create a new email, open Outlook and click on the "New Email" button, which is typically located in the upper left corner of the Home tab. This action opens a new window where you can compose your email.

2. Entering the Recipient's Email Address:

- In the "To" field, enter the email address of the recipient. You can manually type the address or select a contact from your address book by clicking the "To" button. This brings up your contact list, allowing you to choose the desired recipient easily.

- For additional recipients, you can use the "Cc" (carbon copy) and "Bcc" (blind carbon copy) fields. The "Cc" field sends a copy of the email to other recipients, making their addresses visible to all. The "Bcc" field hides the addresses from all recipients, providing privacy.

3. Adding a Subject Line:

- The subject line is crucial as it gives the recipient an idea of the email's content. Ensure the subject is concise, clear, and relevant to the email body. A good subject line improves the chances of your email being read promptly.

4. Writing the Email Body:

- The body of your email is where you convey your message. Start with a greeting, such as "Dear [Name]" or "Hello [Name]," followed by the main content of your email. Keep the following tips in mind:

  - Clarity and Brevity: Be clear and to the point. Avoid unnecessary jargon and long-winded sentences.

  - Paragraphs: Use paragraphs to break up the text. Each paragraph should focus on a single idea.

  - Tone: Maintain a professional tone, especially in business emails. Adjust the tone based on your relationship with the recipient.

  - Proofreading: Always proofread your email for spelling and grammatical errors before sending.

5. Formatting Your Email:

- Outlook provides various formatting tools to enhance the readability and professionalism of your emails. Here are some key formatting options:

- Font Style and Size: Choose a clear, professional font like Arial or Times New Roman. Adjust the size to ensure readability.

- Bold, Italic, Underline: Use these to emphasize important points.

- Bullet Points and Numbered Lists: These are useful for lists and steps, making your email easier to follow.

- Hyperlinks: Insert hyperlinks to provide additional information or references. Highlight the text you want to link, right-click, and select "Hyperlink" to enter the URL.

6. Adding Attachments:

- If you need to include files with your email, click on the "Attach File" button in the ribbon. This opens a dialog box where you can select the file(s) you wish to attach. Outlook supports various file types, including documents, images, and PDFs. Ensure that the attachments are relevant and necessary.

- Attachment Size: Be mindful of the attachment size. Large files can be problematic to send and receive. If necessary, use cloud services like OneDrive or SharePoint to share large files and include a link in the email.

7. Reviewing and Sending Your Email:

- Before sending your email, take a moment to review everything. Check the recipient addresses, subject line, body content, and attachments. Ensure that your email is clear, concise, and free of errors.

- Once you are satisfied, click the "Send" button to dispatch your email. Outlook will send the email to the recipient(s) and move a copy to your "Sent Items" folder for your records.

Advanced Email Creation Techniques:

1. Using Signatures:

- Outlook allows you to create and use signatures to save time and maintain consistency in your emails. A signature typically includes your name, position, company, and contact information. To create a signature:

  - Go to "File" > "Options" > "Mail" > "Signatures."

  - Click "New" to create a new signature and enter your desired information.

- You can create multiple signatures for different purposes and choose the default one for new emails and replies.

2. Templates:

   - If you frequently send similar emails, consider using templates. Templates save time and ensure consistency. To create a template:

      - Compose an email with the desired content and formatting.

      - Click "File" > "Save As" and select "Outlook Template" in the "Save as type" dropdown.

      - To use the template, go to "New Items" > "More Items" > "Choose Form" and select your template from the list.

3. Delayed Sending:

   - Outlook allows you to delay the sending of your emails, which can be useful for scheduling emails to be sent at a later time. To set a delay:

      - In the email composition window, click on "Options" > "Delay Delivery."

      - Check the "Do not deliver before" box and select the desired date and time.

      - Click "Close" and then "Send." The email will be held in your Outbox and sent at the specified time.

4. Using Voting Buttons:

   - Voting buttons are a useful feature for getting quick responses to questions or polls. To add voting buttons:

      - In the email composition window, click on "Options" > "Use Voting Buttons."

      - Choose from the predefined options (e.g., Approve/Reject, Yes/No) or create custom buttons.

      - Recipients can then vote directly from the email, and Outlook will track the responses for you.

5. Automatic Replies:

   - If you are going to be unavailable, setting up automatic replies ensures that senders are informed of your absence. To set up an automatic reply:

      - Go to "File" > "Automatic Replies."

- Select "Send automatic replies" and enter the desired message for both internal and external senders.

- Set the time range for when the replies should be sent, if applicable.

By mastering these steps and techniques, you will be well-equipped to compose and send effective emails using Outlook. Understanding these basics is crucial for beginners and forms the foundation for more advanced email management skills.

3.1.2 Formatting Your Email

Formatting your email properly is crucial to ensure your message is clear, professional, and easy to read. Outlook provides a variety of formatting options that allow you to customize your email's appearance to suit your needs. In this section, we will explore the various formatting tools available in Outlook and how to use them effectively.

Understanding the Formatting Toolbar

The formatting toolbar in Outlook is similar to those found in most word processing programs. It provides options for adjusting font styles, sizes, colors, and other text attributes. Here are some key features of the formatting toolbar:

- Font Style and Size: You can change the font style and size to make your text stand out. Common font styles include Arial, Times New Roman, and Calibri. The font size can be adjusted to make the text larger or smaller.

- Bold, Italic, and Underline: These options allow you to emphasize certain words or phrases. Bold text is thicker and darker, italic text is slanted, and underlined text has a line beneath it.

- Font Color: Changing the font color can help differentiate parts of your email or add emphasis. You can choose from a wide range of colors.

- Highlighting: This tool allows you to highlight text with a background color, similar to using a highlighter pen.

- Bullets and Numbering: You can use bullets or numbering to create lists, which can make your email more organized and easier to read.

- Alignment: Text alignment options include left, center, right, and justified. Left alignment is most common for emails, but you can use other alignments for specific purposes.

- Indentation: Indentation tools help you create indents in your text, useful for block quotes or structured lists.

- Hyperlinks: You can insert hyperlinks to direct the recipient to a website or another email address.

Formatting Text

1. Changing Font Style and Size:

   - To change the font style, select the text you want to modify and choose a font from the font dropdown menu.

   - To change the font size, select the text and choose a size from the font size dropdown menu.

2. Using Bold, Italic, and Underline:

   - Select the text you want to emphasize.

   - Click on the B button for bold, I for italic, or U for underline.

3. Changing Font Color:

   - Select the text you want to change.

   - Click on the font color button and choose a color from the palette.

4. Highlighting Text:

   - Select the text you want to highlight.

   - Click on the highlight button and choose a highlight color.

Creating Lists

1. Bulleted Lists:

   - Click on the bulleted list button.

   - Type your list items. Each time you press Enter, a new bullet point will appear.

2. Numbered Lists:

   - Click on the numbered list button.

   - Type your list items. Each time you press Enter, a new number will appear.

Aligning Text

1. Left Alignment:

   - Select the text you want to align.

   - Click on the left alignment button.

2. Center Alignment:

   - Select the text you want to center.

   - Click on the center alignment button.

3. Right Alignment:

   - Select the text you want to right-align.

   - Click on the right alignment button.

4. Justified Alignment:

   - Select the text you want to justify.

   - Click on the justify alignment button.

Indenting Text

1. Increasing Indent:

   - Select the text you want to indent.

   - Click on the increase indent button.

2. Decreasing Indent:

  - Select the text you want to remove the indent from.

  - Click on the decrease indent button.

Inserting Hyperlinks

1. Creating a Hyperlink:

  - Select the text or image you want to turn into a hyperlink.

  - Click on the hyperlink button.

  - Enter the URL or email address you want to link to and click OK.

Formatting Email Structure

Properly structuring your email helps in conveying your message clearly and effectively. Here are some tips for structuring your email:

1. Subject Line:

  - The subject line should be clear and concise. It should give the recipient an idea of what the email is about.

  - Avoid using all caps or excessive punctuation.

2. Greeting:

  - Start with a polite greeting, such as "Dear [Recipient's Name]" or "Hello [Recipient's Name]".

  - If you don't know the recipient's name, you can use a general greeting like "Dear Sir/Madam" or "To Whom It May Concern".

3. Introduction:

  - Begin with an introduction that provides context for your email.

  - This could be a brief summary of who you are, why you are writing, or what you need from the recipient.

4. Body:

- The body of the email should be organized into clear, concise paragraphs.

- Each paragraph should focus on a single point or idea.

- Use bullet points or numbered lists to break down complex information.

5. Closing:

- End with a polite closing statement, such as "Thank you for your time" or "I look forward to your response".

- Follow with a closing phrase like "Best regards," "Sincerely," or "Yours faithfully," and your name.

6. Signature:

- Include a signature that provides your contact information.

- This typically includes your name, job title, company name, phone number, and email address.

Example of a Well-Formatted Email

Subject: Project Update Meeting

Greeting:

Dear Mr. Johnson,

Introduction:

I hope this email finds you well. I am writing to provide an update on the current status of the XYZ project and to schedule our next meeting to discuss the progress and next steps.

Body:

Project Status:

- We have completed the initial design phase.

- The development team is currently working on the implementation of the main features.

- We are on track to meet the first milestone by the end of this month.

Next Steps:

1. Testing Phase:

  - We plan to start the testing phase on August 1st.

  - The testing will be conducted in three stages: unit testing, integration testing, and system testing.

2. Feedback and Adjustments:

  - We will gather feedback from stakeholders during the testing phase.

  - Any necessary adjustments will be made based on the feedback received.

Meeting Schedule:

Could we schedule a meeting next week to discuss the progress and any potential issues? I am available on Tuesday and Thursday afternoons.

Closing:

Thank you for your attention to this matter. I look forward to discussing the project with you.

Signature:

Best regards,

[Your Name]

[Your Job Title]

[Your Company]

[Your Phone Number]

[Your Email Address]

Tips for Professional Email Formatting

1. Keep it Simple: Avoid using too many fonts, colors, or styles. Stick to one or two fonts and colors to maintain a professional appearance.

2. Be Consistent: Use the same formatting throughout the email to keep it organized and easy to read.

3. Proofread: Always proofread your email for spelling and grammar errors before sending it. A well-written email reflects professionalism.

4. Use Proper Punctuation: Proper punctuation helps convey your message clearly and professionally.

5. Avoid Abbreviations and Slang: Use full words and formal language, especially in professional correspondence.

6. Be Concise: Get to the point quickly and avoid unnecessary information.

By mastering the formatting tools in Outlook and following these guidelines, you can ensure that your emails are clear, professional, and effective. Proper formatting not only helps in conveying your message but also leaves a positive impression on the recipient.

3.1.3 Adding Attachments

Adding attachments to your emails allows you to share files and documents with recipients easily. Whether you need to send a spreadsheet for review or a presentation for a meeting, Outlook simplifies the process of attaching files. Here's how to add attachments effectively:

Step-by-Step Guide to Adding Attachments:

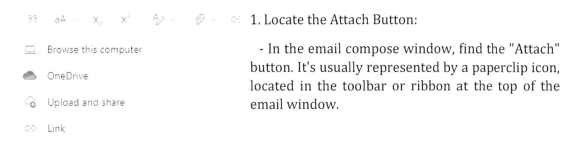

1. Locate the Attach Button:

   - In the email compose window, find the "Attach" button. It's usually represented by a paperclip icon, located in the toolbar or ribbon at the top of the email window.

2. Select Your Files:

   - Click on the "Attach" button. A file dialog box will appear, allowing you to browse your computer or network drives to locate the file you want to attach.

- You can select multiple files by holding down the Ctrl key (Cmd key on Mac) and clicking on each file.

3. Attach the Files:

- Once you've selected the file(s), click on the "Attach" or "Open" button (depending on your operating system).

- Outlook will attach the selected file(s) to your email. You'll see the file names listed under the subject line of your email.

4. Verify Attachments:

- Double-check that all intended files are attached. Each attached file will display a paperclip icon next to its name in the email compose window.

5. Include Attachment Notes (Optional):

- If necessary, you can add a note about the attachments in the body of your email. Simply place your cursor where you want the note to appear and type your message.

6. Send Your Email:

- Once you've completed composing your email and attaching files, proceed to send it by clicking the "Send" button.

Tips for Attaching Files in Outlook:

- File Size Limits: Be aware of any file size limits set by your email provider or organization. If your attachment exceeds the limit, consider using cloud storage or compressing the file.

- File Types: Outlook supports a wide range of file types for attachments, including documents, images, spreadsheets, and presentations. Ensure your recipients can open the file types you send.

- Naming Conventions: Use clear and concise file names for attachments to help recipients identify the content easily.

Best Practices:

- Security Awareness: Exercise caution when opening attachments from unknown sources to avoid potential security risks.

- Inline Attachments: Outlook allows you to insert images and files directly into the body of your email. Explore this feature for a more integrated presentation of your content.

By mastering the skill of attaching files in Outlook, you can enhance your communication efficiency and ensure that your recipients receive all necessary documents and information promptly.

3.2 Receiving and Reading Emails

3.2.1 Inbox Overview

Upon opening your Outlook inbox, you enter the hub of your email activity. The inbox is where all incoming emails are initially displayed, awaiting your attention. Understanding how to efficiently manage and navigate your inbox is crucial for staying organized and responsive in your communication.

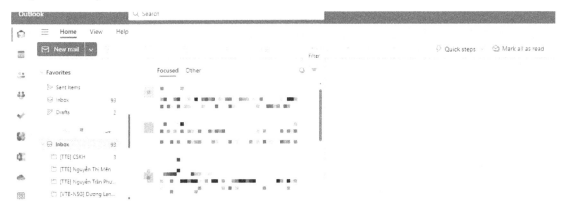

Layout and Components

The inbox interface typically consists of several key elements designed to streamline your email management:

1. Email List: This central area displays a list of emails received, showing essential details such as sender, subject, and timestamp. Each email is represented as a separate entry in the list, allowing you to quickly scan through incoming messages.

2. Reading Pane: Adjacent to the email list, the reading pane provides a preview of the selected email's content without needing to open it fully. This preview helps you assess the importance of emails at a glance, enabling quicker decision-making on which emails to prioritize.

3. Sort and Filter Options: Outlook offers various sorting and filtering options to organize your inbox according to your preferences. You can sort emails by date, sender, subject, or other criteria, making it easier to find specific messages or focus on recent communications.

4. Search Functionality: Located prominently at the top of the inbox, the search bar allows you to quickly locate emails using keywords, sender names, or other search criteria. This feature is invaluable for retrieving specific information buried within a large volume of emails.

5. Reading and Management Tools: Icons and buttons above the email list provide essential tools for reading and managing emails. These tools include options to reply, forward, delete, archive, mark as unread, or flag emails for follow-up.

Customization Options

Outlook provides several customization options to tailor your inbox experience to suit your workflow:

- View Settings: You can adjust the layout and appearance of your inbox using view settings. Options include changing the arrangement of email columns, adjusting the size of the reading pane, or choosing different themes for visual customization.

- Conversation View: Enabling conversation view groups related emails into threads, making it easier to track and manage ongoing conversations with multiple replies.

Best Practices for Inbox Management

Efficient inbox management is crucial for maintaining productivity and responsiveness:

- Regular Maintenance: Schedule regular times to review and clean up your inbox. Archive or delete old emails that are no longer needed to keep your inbox clutter-free.

- Use Folders and Categories: Organize emails into folders based on projects, clients, or topics for easier retrieval and reference. Use categories to label and prioritize emails within your inbox.

- Respond Timely: Aim to respond promptly to important emails to maintain effective communication and avoid backlog.

By mastering the inbox overview and implementing these best practices, you can optimize your email management workflow in Outlook, ensuring that you stay organized and efficient in handling your incoming messages.

This detailed overview equips you with the knowledge to navigate and utilize your Outlook inbox effectively, enhancing your overall productivity and communication efficiency.

3.2.2 Reading Pane Options

The Reading Pane in Outlook is a crucial feature that allows users to preview and read emails without opening them in a separate window. This functionality enhances productivity by enabling quick access to email content and various actions. Let's delve into the different options and settings available within the Reading Pane to optimize your email reading experience.

1. Viewing Emails in the Reading Pane

By default, the Reading Pane is located on the right side of the Outlook window, but you can also place it at the bottom or turn it off entirely. To customize the Reading Pane's placement:

1. Go to the View tab on the ribbon.

2. In the Layout group, click on Reading Pane.

3. Choose from the options: Right, Bottom, or Off.

The Right option provides a vertical split, displaying the email list on the left and the email content on the right. The Bottom option offers a horizontal split, with the email list on top and the email content below. Adjust the layout based on your preference and screen size.

2. Reading Pane Settings

Outlook offers various settings to customize how emails appear in the Reading Pane:

- Mark as Read: By default, Outlook marks an email as read after you select it and view it in the Reading Pane for a certain duration. You can change this behavior to suit your needs. To do this:

  1. Go to File > Options.

  2. Select Mail.

3. In the Outlook Panes section, click Reading Pane.

4. Adjust the settings for marking items as read, such as the delay before marking an item as read or choosing not to mark items as read when viewed in the Reading Pane.

- Single Key Reading: Enable single-key reading using the spacebar to move through your emails quickly. This feature is particularly useful for efficiently navigating through long messages or multiple emails. To enable it:

1. Go to File > Options.

2. Select Mail.

3. In the Outlook Panes section, click Reading Pane.

4. Check the box for Single key reading using space bar.

3. Adjusting the Reading Pane Width

The Reading Pane's width can be adjusted to provide more space for reading emails or to show more of the email list. To adjust the width:

1. Hover your cursor over the border between the Reading Pane and the email list.

2. When the cursor changes to a double-sided arrow, click and drag the border to resize the pane.

4. Displaying Message Headers

Message headers contain essential information about the email, such as the sender, recipient, subject, and timestamp. By default, the Reading Pane shows a condensed view of the message header, but you can expand it to see more details:

1. Click the Expand/Collapse arrow next to the message header in the Reading Pane.

2. This action reveals additional fields like CC, BCC, and full email addresses.

5. Handling Attachments in the Reading Pane

Attachments are an integral part of many emails. The Reading Pane allows you to interact with attachments without opening the email fully:

- Preview Attachments: If the attachment is a common file type (e.g., PDF, Word document), you can preview it directly in the Reading Pane. Click on the attachment to open the preview.

- Download Attachments: Right-click the attachment and select Save As to download it to your computer.

- Open Attachments: Double-click the attachment to open it in its respective application.

6. Quick Actions in the Reading Pane

Outlook provides several quick action buttons within the Reading Pane for efficient email management. These actions include replying, forwarding, deleting, and flagging emails. The buttons are typically located at the top of the Reading Pane, providing easy access:

- Reply and Forward: Click Reply or Forward to compose a response or forward the email without leaving the Reading Pane.

- Delete: Click the Delete button to move the email to the Deleted Items folder.

- Flag: Use the Flag button to mark the email for follow-up.

7. Reading Pane in Different Email Views

Outlook supports various email views, and the Reading Pane can be used in each view to enhance your workflow:

- Compact View: This is the default view, where emails are listed compactly with the Reading Pane displaying the selected email's content.

- Single View: In this view, each email occupies a single line in the list, and the Reading Pane shows the content. It's suitable for users who prefer a more streamlined appearance.

- Preview View: This view shows a preview of the email content directly in the list, with the Reading Pane providing a more detailed view. It's ideal for quickly skimming through emails.

8. Customizing the Reading Pane for Accessibility

Outlook includes several accessibility features to enhance the reading experience for all users, including those with visual impairments:

- Zoom: Adjust the zoom level in the Reading Pane to make the text larger or smaller. Use the zoom slider at the bottom right corner of the Outlook window.

- High Contrast Mode: Enable high contrast mode to improve text readability. This can be set in Windows settings, and Outlook will follow suit.

- Screen Reader Compatibility: Outlook is compatible with screen readers, providing auditory feedback for email content.

9. Troubleshooting Reading Pane Issues

Occasionally, you might encounter issues with the Reading Pane not displaying content correctly. Here are some troubleshooting steps:

- Restart Outlook: Close and reopen Outlook to reset the Reading Pane.

- Update Outlook: Ensure you have the latest updates installed for Outlook to avoid bugs and compatibility issues.

- Reset View Settings: If the Reading Pane behaves unexpectedly, reset the view settings:

  1. Go to the View tab.

  2. In the Current View group, click Reset View.

- Disable Add-ins: Some add-ins might interfere with the Reading Pane. Disable add-ins to see if the issue is resolved:

  1. Go to File > Options.

  2. Select Add-ins.

  3. Manage COM Add-ins and disable any add-ins causing problems.

By understanding and utilizing these Reading Pane options, you can significantly improve your email management efficiency in Outlook. The ability to preview, read, and interact with emails directly in the Reading Pane streamlines your workflow, making it easier to handle large volumes of emails and stay organized. Adjust the settings to fit your preferences and optimize your email reading experience.

3.3 Organizing Your Emails

3.3.1 Folders

Organizing emails effectively is a key aspect of managing your inbox efficiently. In Outlook, folders play a crucial role in helping you categorize, store, and retrieve emails with ease. This section will guide you through the process of creating, managing, and using folders to keep your emails organized.

Creating Folders

Creating folders in Outlook is a straightforward process. Folders can be customized to suit your organizational needs, allowing you to sort emails by project, client, topic, or any other criteria that make sense for your workflow.

1. Creating a New Folder:

   - Step 1: Open Outlook and navigate to the left-hand sidebar where your email accounts and folders are listed.

   - Step 2: Right-click on the email account or an existing folder under which you want to create the new folder.

   - Step 3: Select "New Folder" from the context menu that appears.

   - Step 4: A text box will appear. Enter the name for your new folder and press "Enter."

2. Best Practices for Naming Folders:

   - Use clear, descriptive names that indicate the content or purpose of the folder. For example, "Project X Updates" or "Client Invoices."

   - Avoid overly long names to keep the sidebar tidy and readable.

   - Use a consistent naming convention for similar types of folders, such as prefixing project-related folders with "Proj-" (e.g., "Proj-Website Redesign").

Managing Folders

Once you have created folders, the next step is to manage them effectively. This includes organizing folders hierarchically, renaming them as needed, and moving or deleting folders when they are no longer necessary.

1. Organizing Folders:

   - Subfolders: To create a subfolder, right-click on the parent folder and select "New Folder." This is useful for creating nested categories within a larger category. For example, under a folder named "Projects," you could create subfolders for each specific project.

   - Hierarchy: Organize your folders in a hierarchical structure that mirrors your workflow. For example:

   - Projects

     - Project A

     - Project B

   - Clients

     - Client 1

     - Client 2

2. Renaming Folders:

   - Step 1: Right-click on the folder you wish to rename.

   - Step 2: Select "Rename Folder" from the context menu.

   - Step 3: Enter the new name and press "Enter."

3. Moving Folders:

   - Drag and Drop: Click and hold the folder you want to move, drag it to the desired location, and release the mouse button.

   - Context Menu: Right-click the folder, select "Move Folder," and choose the destination from the list of available folders.

4. Deleting Folders:

   - Step 1: Right-click on the folder you wish to delete.

   - Step 2: Select "Delete Folder" from the context menu.

- Step 3: Confirm the deletion if prompted. Note that deleting a folder will also delete all emails contained within it.

Using Folders to Organize Emails

Folders are most effective when they are used consistently to sort and store emails. Here are some strategies for using folders to keep your inbox organized:

1. Manual Sorting:

  - Drag and Drop: Move emails to folders manually by dragging them from the inbox and dropping them into the appropriate folder.

  - Context Menu: Right-click an email, select "Move," and choose the target folder from the list.

2. Automatic Sorting with Rules:

  - Creating Rules: Outlook allows you to create rules that automatically sort incoming emails based on criteria you define. For example, you can create a rule to move all emails from a specific sender to a designated folder.

    - Step 1: Go to the "Home" tab and click on "Rules" in the "Move" group.

    - Step 2: Select "Manage Rules & Alerts" to open the Rules and Alerts window.

    - Step 3: Click "New Rule" and follow the wizard to define the criteria and action for the rule.

  - Managing Rules: Regularly review and update your rules to ensure they continue to meet your needs as your email volume and patterns change.

3. Using Search Folders:

  - What Are Search Folders? Search folders are virtual folders that show email items matching specific search criteria. They do not move emails but provide a way to view emails that meet certain conditions.

  - Creating Search Folders:

    - Step 1: Go to the "Folder" tab and click "New Search Folder."

- Step 2: Choose from the predefined search criteria or create a custom search folder with specific conditions.

  - Examples of Search Folders:

    - "Unread Mail" to see all unread emails.

    - "Mail from Specific People" to view emails from specific contacts.

Tips for Effective Folder Management

1. Keep It Simple: Avoid creating too many folders, as this can make it difficult to find emails quickly. Aim for a balance between comprehensive categorization and simplicity.

2. Review Regularly: Periodically review your folder structure to ensure it still meets your needs. Consolidate or eliminate folders that are no longer necessary.

3. Archive Old Emails: Use an archive folder to store old emails that you do not need regularly but want to keep for reference. This helps keep your active folders uncluttered.

4. Stay Consistent: Develop a routine for sorting and filing emails, whether it's immediately upon receipt, at the end of each day, or weekly. Consistency is key to maintaining an organized inbox.

By effectively utilizing folders, you can keep your Outlook inbox organized, improve your efficiency in managing emails, and ensure that important messages are easily accessible when needed.

3.3.2 Categories

Organizing your emails can greatly enhance your productivity and help you manage your inbox more efficiently. One of the most powerful tools Outlook offers for email organization is the use of categories. Categories allow you to tag and color-code your emails, making it easier to identify and prioritize messages based on their content or importance. In this section, we will delve into the various aspects of using categories in Outlook, including how to create, manage, and effectively utilize them.

What Are Categories?

Categories in Outlook are a versatile feature that allows you to label and color-code emails, calendar events, tasks, and contacts. Each category can be assigned a specific name and color, enabling you to quickly identify and sort your items based on these visual cues. Categories are customizable, meaning you can create categories that fit your specific needs and preferences.

Creating Categories

To start using categories, you first need to create them. Here's a step-by-step guide on how to create categories in Outlook:

1. Open Outlook: Launch your Outlook application and navigate to the main screen where you can see your emails.

2. Open the Categorize Menu: In the Home tab on the Ribbon, locate the Tags group and click on the "Categorize" button.

3. Manage Categories: In the drop-down menu, select "All Categories." This will open the Color Categories dialog box.

4. Create a New Category: Click on the "New" button to create a new category.

5. Name and Color: In the Add New Category dialog box, enter a name for your category. Choose a color that will be associated with this category from the color palette.

6. Shortcut Key (Optional): If desired, you can assign a shortcut key to your category for quick access.

7. Save Your Category: Click "OK" to save your new category. It will now appear in the list of available categories.

Repeat these steps to create as many categories as you need. For instance, you might create categories like "Important," "Work," "Personal," "Follow Up," and "Project X."

Assigning Categories to Emails

Once you have created your categories, the next step is to assign them to your emails. Here's how you can do this:

1. Select an Email: Click on the email you want to categorize.

2. Categorize: In the Home tab, click on the "Categorize" button in the Tags group.

3. Choose a Category: Select the category you want to assign to the email from the drop-down list. The email will now be tagged with the chosen category color and label.

You can also assign multiple categories to a single email if it falls under more than one category. For example, an email related to a work project that is also urgent can be categorized as both "Work" and "Important."

Viewing and Sorting Emails by Categories

After assigning categories to your emails, you can use them to view and sort your inbox more effectively. Here are some methods to do this:

1. Category Column: Ensure that the Category column is visible in your email list view. If it is not, you can add it by right-clicking on the column headers, selecting "View Settings," then "Columns," and adding "Categories" to the list of displayed columns.

2. Sort by Category: Click on the Category column header to sort your emails by category. This will group emails with the same category together, making it easier to focus on specific types of emails.

3. Search by Category: Use the Search bar in Outlook to filter emails by category. Type "category:" followed by the category name (e.g., "category:Important") to display only emails with that category.

Customizing Categories

Categories in Outlook are highly customizable, allowing you to tailor them to your specific workflow. Here are some customization tips:

1. Rename Categories: If you want to change the name of a category, go to the Categorize menu, select "All Categories," and then click on the category you want to rename. Enter the new name and click "OK."

2. Change Category Colors: You can also change the color of a category by selecting it in the Color Categories dialog box and choosing a new color from the palette.

3. Delete Categories: If a category is no longer needed, you can delete it by selecting it in the Color Categories dialog box and clicking the "Delete" button. Note that deleting a category will remove it from all items it was assigned to.

Best Practices for Using Categories

To get the most out of categories in Outlook, consider the following best practices:

1. Consistent Naming Conventions: Use consistent and descriptive names for your categories. This will help you quickly identify the purpose of each category.

2. Color Coding: Choose distinct colors for each category to avoid confusion. Bright and easily distinguishable colors work best.

3. Regular Review: Periodically review your categories to ensure they still meet your needs. Update or delete categories as necessary.

4. Combine with Other Tools: Use categories in conjunction with other Outlook features such as folders, flags, and rules to create a robust email management system.

5. Training and Communication: If you are using categories in a work environment, ensure that all team members understand the category system and use it consistently.

Practical Examples of Using Categories

To illustrate the effectiveness of categories, let's look at some practical examples:

- Project Management: Create categories for each project you are working on (e.g., "Project A," "Project B"). Assign emails related to each project to the corresponding category. This allows you to quickly view all emails related to a specific project by sorting or searching by category.

- Priority Levels: Use categories to indicate the priority of emails (e.g., "High Priority," "Medium Priority," "Low Priority"). This helps you focus on the most critical emails first.

- Personal vs. Work: Separate your personal and work emails by categorizing them as "Personal" and "Work." This can help maintain a clear distinction between your professional and personal correspondence.

Using Categories Beyond Emails

Categories are not limited to emails; you can also use them for other Outlook items such as calendar events, tasks, and contacts. Here's how:

1. Calendar Events: Assign categories to calendar events to color-code your schedule. For example, use different colors for work meetings, personal appointments, and deadlines.

2. Tasks: Categorize tasks to prioritize and organize your to-do list. You can categorize tasks by project, priority, or type of work.

3. Contacts: Use categories to group contacts based on their relationship to you (e.g., "Family," "Friends," "Work Colleagues").

By extending the use of categories to other Outlook items, you can create a cohesive organizational system that spans your entire Outlook environment.

Conclusion

Categories are a powerful feature in Outlook that can significantly enhance your ability to organize and manage your emails and other items. By creating custom categories, assigning them to your emails, and using them to sort and view your messages, you can maintain a more organized and efficient inbox. Implementing best practices and customizing categories to fit your workflow will ensure that you get the most out of this feature. Whether you are managing a busy work schedule or keeping track of personal emails, categories provide a versatile and effective solution for email organization.

3.3.3 Flags and Reminders

Flags and reminders are powerful tools in Outlook that help you manage your emails more effectively. They serve as visual cues and alerts to ensure that important emails are not overlooked and are acted upon in a timely manner. This section will cover the basics of using flags and reminders, their benefits, and how to integrate them into your daily email management routine.

Using Flags

Flags in Outlook can be used to mark emails that require follow-up or action. When you flag an email, it is highlighted and added to your to-do list, making it easier to track and prioritize your tasks.

Adding a Flag to an Email

1. Select the Email: Open your inbox and select the email you want to flag.

2. Flag Icon: Look for the flag icon in the email list. It usually appears to the right of the email subject line.

3. Click the Flag: Click the flag icon. This will add a flag to the email, indicating that it requires follow-up.

Customizing Flags

Outlook allows you to customize flags to better suit your needs. You can set different flags for different follow-up times, such as today, tomorrow, this week, or next week.

1. Right-Click the Flag: Right-click on the flag icon next to the email.

2. Choose Follow-Up: From the context menu, hover over "Follow Up."

3. Select Time Frame: Choose a time frame from the list, such as "Today," "Tomorrow," "This Week," "Next Week," "No Date," or "Custom."

4. Custom Date: If you select "Custom," a dialog box will appear where you can set a specific date and time for the follow-up.

Viewing Flagged Emails

To keep track of all your flagged emails, Outlook provides several ways to view them:

1. To-Do List: Go to the "Tasks" pane. Here, you will find a list of all flagged emails along with other tasks.

2. Search Folder: Outlook has a built-in search folder called "For Follow Up" that aggregates all flagged emails in one place. You can find this folder in the navigation pane under "Search Folders."

Using Reminders

Reminders in Outlook are notifications that alert you to follow up on flagged emails or tasks at a specific time. They are similar to alarms and can be set to ensure that you don't miss important deadlines.

Setting a Reminder

1. Select the Email: Choose the email you want to set a reminder for.

2. Right-Click the Flag: Right-click on the flag icon next to the email.

3. Add Reminder: From the context menu, select "Add Reminder."

4. Set Date and Time: In the dialog box that appears, set the date and time when you want to be reminded.

5. Click OK: Click "OK" to save the reminder.

Managing Reminders

Outlook allows you to manage your reminders to ensure that they fit into your schedule:

1. View Reminders: Reminders will pop up at the specified time. You can view them in the "Reminders" window, which appears on your screen.

2. Snooze or Dismiss: When a reminder pops up, you can choose to "Snooze" it for a specified period or "Dismiss" it if the task is complete.

3. Edit Reminder: To change the reminder time, right-click on the flagged email, select "Add Reminder," and adjust the date and time as needed.

Benefits of Using Flags and Reminders

1. Increased Productivity: Flags and reminders help you stay organized and ensure that important emails and tasks are not forgotten.

2. Better Time Management: By setting specific follow-up times, you can manage your time more effectively and prioritize your tasks.

3. Improved Follow-Up: Flags and reminders provide a visual and audible cue to follow up on emails, improving your responsiveness and reliability.

Integrating Flags and Reminders into Your Workflow

To make the most of flags and reminders, consider integrating them into your daily email management routine:

1. Daily Review: At the beginning of each day, review your flagged emails and set reminders for any that require action. This will help you prioritize your tasks and ensure that nothing falls through the cracks.

2. Categorize Flags: Use different flag colors or labels to categorize emails by priority or type of follow-up needed. For example, use red flags for urgent tasks and blue flags for routine follow-ups.

3. Regular Updates: Regularly update and review your flagged emails and reminders. Mark tasks as complete when done and adjust reminder times as needed to reflect your changing priorities.

4. Synchronization: If you use Outlook across multiple devices, ensure that your flagged emails and reminders are synchronized. This way, you can access your to-do list and receive reminders regardless of which device you are using.

Example Scenarios

To illustrate the practical use of flags and reminders, consider the following scenarios:

Scenario 1: Following Up on a Client Email

You receive an email from a client requesting a proposal by the end of the week.

1. Flag the Email: Flag the email for follow-up "This Week."

2. Set Reminder: Set a reminder for two days before the deadline to start working on the proposal.

3. Review To-Do List: Check your to-do list daily to ensure you are on track to complete the task on time.

4. Follow-Up: On the reminder date, start working on the proposal and send it to the client by the deadline.

Scenario 2: Scheduling a Team Meeting

You need to schedule a team meeting to discuss a new project.

1. Flag the Email: Flag the initial email discussion for follow-up "Tomorrow."

2. Set Reminder: Set a reminder for tomorrow morning to send out a meeting invitation.

3. Send Invitation: When the reminder pops up, send the meeting invitation to your team.

4. Follow-Up: Use the flag to remind yourself to confirm attendance and prepare an agenda.

Conclusion

Flags and reminders are essential tools in Outlook that help you stay organized and ensure timely follow-up on important emails and tasks. By effectively using flags and reminders, you can enhance your productivity, manage your time better, and improve your overall email management experience. Integrate these tools into your daily routine and customize them to fit your specific needs, ensuring that you never miss a critical task or deadline.

CHAPTER IV
Working with Contacts

4.1 Creating and Managing Contacts

4.1.1 Adding New Contacts

Adding new contacts in Outlook is a fundamental task that allows you to keep track of important people in your personal and professional life. The process is straightforward but understanding each step thoroughly ensures you make the most of Outlook's contact management features.

Step-by-Step Guide to Adding New Contacts in Outlook

1. Open the Contacts Section:

   - Launch Outlook.

   - In the lower-left corner of the Outlook window, click on the "People" icon. This opens the Contacts section, where you can view, create, and manage your contacts.

2. Create a New Contact:

   - In the Home tab, located in the Ribbon at the top of the window, click on the "New Contact" button. This action opens a new contact form.

3. Enter Contact Information:

   - Full Name: In the contact form, you'll see fields for entering the contact's first name, last name, and, optionally, middle name and title. It's essential to fill these fields accurately for easy identification.

- Company: Enter the company name if applicable. This field helps organize contacts, especially in a business context.

- Job Title: Add the contact's job title. This information can be particularly useful for business contacts.

- Email Addresses: Outlook allows you to store multiple email addresses for a single contact. Enter the primary email in the "Email" field. For additional email addresses, click on the down arrow next to the Email field to reveal "Email 2" and "Email 3" options.

- Phone Numbers: Add phone numbers by selecting the appropriate type from the drop-down menu (e.g., Business, Home, Mobile). You can store multiple phone numbers for each contact.

- Address: Enter the contact's address. You can specify different types of addresses, such as Business, Home, and Other. Click "Details" to add more specific address information, including city, state, zip code, and country.

- Notes: Use the "Notes" section to add any additional information about the contact. This can include personal notes, important dates, or any other relevant details.

4. Categorize the Contact:

- Outlook allows you to categorize contacts by assigning them color-coded categories. Click on the "Categorize" button in the Ribbon, and select the appropriate category. Categories help you organize and find contacts more efficiently.

5. Save and Close:

- After entering all the necessary information, click the "Save & Close" button in the Ribbon. This action saves the contact to your address book.

Additional Features and Tips for Adding Contacts

- Contact Pictures:

- You can add a picture to each contact. Click on the photo icon in the contact form, and upload an image from your computer. This feature helps in visually identifying contacts quickly.

- Social Network Integration:

- Outlook can connect to social networks like LinkedIn. By linking your social media accounts, Outlook can automatically update contact information based on their social network profiles. To set this up, go to "File" > "Account Settings" > "Social Network Accounts".

- Linking Contacts:

- If you have duplicate entries for a single person, you can link these contacts. Open one of the contact entries, click "Link Contacts" in the Ribbon, and select the duplicate contact to link them.

- Custom Fields:

- If the standard fields are insufficient, you can create custom fields. Go to the "All Fields" tab in the contact form, select "User-defined fields in this item," and click "New" to add a custom field. This feature is useful for storing additional, specific information.

- Keyboard Shortcuts:

- For quicker contact entry, use keyboard shortcuts. For example, press "Ctrl+Shift+C" to create a new contact, and "Ctrl+S" to save a contact.

Best Practices for Adding Contacts

1. Consistency:

- Maintain a consistent format for entering names, addresses, and other details. Consistency helps in searching and sorting contacts efficiently.

2. Complete Information:

- Always try to fill in as much information as possible. Even if some details seem irrelevant now, they might be useful later.

3. Regular Updates:

- Periodically review and update your contact information to ensure it remains current. Outdated contact details can lead to communication breakdowns.

4. Use Descriptive Notes:

- Utilize the notes section for additional context about the contact. This could include how you met them, topics of interest, or important dates.

Benefits of Proper Contact Management

- Improved Communication:

  - Accurate and complete contact information ensures effective communication, reducing the chances of errors or missed opportunities.

- Time Efficiency:

  - Well-organized contacts save time. You can quickly find the person you need to contact, leading to improved productivity.

- Professionalism:

  - Having up-to-date and detailed contact information portrays professionalism. It ensures that you are always prepared for interactions, whether in personal or business contexts.

Troubleshooting Common Issues

1. Duplicate Contacts:

  - If you notice duplicates, use the "Clean Up Contacts" feature in Outlook. Go to "File" > "Options" > "Advanced" > "Export," and select "Import/Export" to remove duplicates.

2. Sync Issues:

  - Ensure your internet connection is stable if you face issues syncing contacts with other devices or applications. Check Outlook settings to ensure proper sync configuration.

3. Lost Contacts:

  - If contacts are missing, check the Deleted Items folder. Contacts might have been accidentally deleted. If not found, use the Outlook recovery tool to restore lost data.

By following these steps and tips, you can efficiently add and manage your contacts in Outlook, ensuring your address book is always organized and up-to-date. This foundational skill will greatly enhance your overall Outlook experience, making communication smoother and more effective.

4.1.2 Editing Contact Information

Editing contact information in Outlook is a crucial task to ensure that your address book remains accurate and up-to-date. Whether it's changing a phone number, updating an email address, or adding new details, the process is straightforward and user-friendly. This section will guide you through the steps involved in editing contact information, offering tips and best practices along the way.

Accessing the Contact List

Before you can edit a contact's information, you need to access your contact list. Here's how to do it:

1. Open Outlook: Start by launching Outlook. Ensure you are signed in to the correct account.

2. Navigate to Contacts: Click on the "People" icon, usually found at the bottom of the navigation pane. This will open your contact list.

3. Search for the Contact: If you have a large number of contacts, you can use the search bar at the top to quickly find the contact you want to edit. Type in the name, email address, or any relevant detail to locate the contact.

Editing Contact Information

Once you have located the contact, follow these steps to edit their information:

1. Select the Contact: Click on the contact's name to open their details.

2. Edit Mode: Click on the "Edit" button or icon, which is typically represented by a pencil or the word "Edit" at the top of the contact's details pane.

3. Update Information: You will now be in the edit mode, where you can update various fields. Here are some common fields you might need to edit:

- Name: If the contact's name has changed, you can update their first name, last name, and any middle names or initials.

- Email Addresses: Add, remove, or update email addresses. Outlook allows you to store multiple email addresses for each contact, such as work and personal emails.

- Phone Numbers: Update phone numbers, including mobile, home, work, and other types.

- Company Details: If the contact's employment information has changed, update the company name, job title, and department.

- Physical Address: Edit or add home, work, or other addresses.

- Birthday and Anniversary: Update important dates that Outlook can remind you about.

- Notes: Add any notes about the contact that might be useful, such as how you met, special instructions, or personal preferences.

4. Save Changes: After making the necessary updates, click the "Save" button to ensure that your changes are stored.

Advanced Editing Features

Outlook provides several advanced features for managing contact information effectively. Here are some you might find useful:

- Custom Fields: If the standard fields are not enough, you can create custom fields to store additional information unique to your needs.

- Categories: Assign categories to your contacts to organize them into groups. This is especially useful for managing large contact lists.

- Photos: Add or update a contact's photo to make it easier to identify them at a glance.

- Social Media Profiles: Include links to your contacts' social media profiles, such as LinkedIn, Twitter, or Facebook.

Best Practices for Maintaining Contact Information

To keep your contact list efficient and useful, consider the following best practices:

1. Regular Updates: Periodically review and update contact information to ensure accuracy. This is particularly important for business contacts where information can change frequently.

2. Use Complete Information: Whenever possible, fill in all relevant fields for each contact. The more information you have, the more useful your contacts will be.

3. Consistent Formatting: Use consistent formats for phone numbers, addresses, and other data to make searching and sorting easier.

4. Backup Your Contacts: Regularly backup your contact list to prevent data loss. This can be done by exporting your contacts to a file or using cloud storage options.

5. Merge Duplicates: Over time, you might end up with duplicate contacts. Use Outlook's merge feature to combine duplicate entries and avoid clutter.

Troubleshooting Common Issues

Occasionally, you might encounter issues while editing contact information. Here are some common problems and their solutions:

1. Changes Not Saving: If your changes are not saving, ensure you are clicking the "Save" button after making edits. Also, check your internet connection if you are using a cloud-based Outlook service.

2. Contact Not Found: If you cannot find a contact, double-check your search criteria. Make sure you are searching in the correct contact folder if you have multiple folders.

3. Synchronization Issues: If you are using Outlook on multiple devices, make sure your contacts are synchronized across all devices. Check your sync settings and ensure you are signed in to the same account on all devices.

Using Outlook Mobile App

Editing contact information on the go is made easy with the Outlook mobile app. Here's how you can manage contacts using the mobile app:

1. Open the App: Launch the Outlook app on your mobile device.

2. Access Contacts: Tap on the "Contacts" icon or navigate to the "People" section.

3. Select and Edit: Find and select the contact you want to edit. Tap the "Edit" button to update their information.

4. Save Changes: After making the necessary updates, tap "Save" to store your changes.

The mobile app offers similar features to the desktop version, allowing you to manage your contacts efficiently no matter where you are.

Conclusion

Editing contact information in Outlook is a straightforward process that helps ensure your address book is always up-to-date and accurate. By following the steps outlined in this section, you can easily manage and update your contacts, keeping your communication efficient and organized. Remember to regularly review and update your contacts, use consistent formatting, and take advantage of Outlook's advanced features to get the most out of your contact list. With these practices, you'll maintain a well-organized and effective contact management system, making your Outlook experience even more productive.

4.2 Using Contact Groups

Managing a large number of contacts can become cumbersome, especially when you need to send emails to the same group of people frequently. This is where contact groups, also known as distribution lists, come in handy. By creating contact groups in Outlook, you can simplify the process of communicating with multiple contacts at once. In this section, we will explore how to create and manage contact groups to enhance your email efficiency.

4.2.1 Creating Contact Groups

Creating a contact group in Outlook is a straightforward process that involves a few simple steps. Follow these instructions to set up your contact groups effectively:

1. Open Outlook: Launch Outlook on your computer and navigate to the "Home" tab if you are not already there.

2. Access the Contacts Section: Click on the "People" or "Contacts" icon, usually located at the bottom of the navigation pane. This will open the Contacts view where you can see all your individual contacts and contact groups.

3. Create a New Contact Group: In the Contacts view, go to the "Home" tab and look for the "New Contact Group" button. Click on it to start creating a new contact group.

4. Name Your Contact Group: A new window will open, allowing you to name your contact group. Choose a name that is descriptive and easy to remember. For example, if you are creating a group for your marketing team, you might name it "Marketing Team".

5. Add Members to Your Contact Group: Now, it's time to add members to your contact group. There are several ways to do this:

   - From Your Contacts: Click on the "Add Members" button and select "From Outlook Contacts" or "From Address Book". This will open a dialog box where you can search for and select the contacts you want to add to the group. Select the desired contacts and click "Members" to add them to the group.

   - New Email Contact: If you want to add someone who is not already in your contacts, select "New E-mail Contact" from the "Add Members" dropdown. Enter the email address and name of the new contact, and then click "OK" to add them to the group.

6. Review and Save Your Contact Group: Once you have added all the desired members, review the list to ensure accuracy. You can remove any contacts by selecting them and clicking the "Remove Member" button. After reviewing, click "Save & Close" to finalize and save your new contact group.

7. Using Your Contact Group: Your newly created contact group will now appear in your Contacts list. To send an email to the group, simply create a new email message, enter the name of the contact group in the "To" field, and Outlook will automatically populate the email addresses of all group members.

Adding and Removing Members

Managing the members of a contact group is an ongoing task, especially as team compositions and contact lists change over time. Here's how to add and remove members from an existing contact group:

1. Editing a Contact Group: To edit a contact group, go to the "People" or "Contacts" section in Outlook, and double-click on the contact group you want to modify. This will open the group in a new window.

2. Adding Members: Click on the "Add Members" button and choose the appropriate option (From Outlook Contacts, From Address Book, or New E-mail Contact). Select the contacts you wish to add and confirm the addition.

3. Removing Members: To remove a member from the group, select their name in the group members list and click the "Remove Member" button. This will immediately remove the selected contact from the group.

4. Saving Changes: After making the necessary changes, click "Save & Close" to update the contact group.

Utilizing Contact Groups Effectively

To make the most of contact groups in Outlook, consider the following tips:

1. Group Naming Conventions: Use clear and consistent naming conventions for your contact groups. This will help you quickly identify and select the right group when composing emails. For example, you might use prefixes like "Team_", "Project_", or "Dept_" to categorize your groups.

2. Regular Updates: Periodically review and update your contact groups to ensure they reflect the current composition of your teams or projects. Remove outdated contacts and add new members as needed.

3. Sub-Groups: For larger teams or projects, consider creating sub-groups for more specific communication needs. For example, within a "Marketing Team" group, you might have sub-groups like "Marketing Managers", "Content Creators", and "Designers".

4. Group Communication: Encourage group communication by using the contact group for regular updates, announcements, and collaborative efforts. This can improve team cohesion and ensure everyone is on the same page.

5. Bcc for Large Groups: When sending emails to large contact groups, consider using the Bcc (blind carbon copy) field to protect the privacy of group members and avoid exposing their email addresses to everyone.

Troubleshooting Contact Group Issues

Despite the convenience of contact groups, you may encounter some common issues. Here are a few troubleshooting tips:

1. Group Not Found: If Outlook does not recognize your contact group when you type its name in the "To" field, ensure that the group name is correct and that it exists in your Contacts list.

2. Members Not Receiving Emails: If some group members report that they are not receiving emails, check their email addresses for accuracy in the group list. Ensure that there are no typos or outdated addresses.

3. Duplicate Groups: Avoid creating duplicate contact groups with similar names, as this can lead to confusion. If you accidentally create duplicates, consolidate them into a single group and delete the extras.

4. Email Limits: Be aware of email sending limits set by your email service provider. Sending emails to very large groups may trigger these limits, resulting in delivery failures. If necessary, divide your contact group into smaller segments.

Conclusion

Using contact groups in Outlook is a powerful way to streamline your communication and manage large numbers of contacts efficiently. By following the steps outlined in this section, you can create, manage, and utilize contact groups to enhance your productivity and ensure effective communication within your teams and projects. Remember to regularly review and update your contact groups to keep them accurate and relevant, and make use of the tips and troubleshooting advice to avoid common issues. With well-organized contact groups, you can save time and effort in your email management, allowing you to focus on more important tasks.

4.2.2 Managing Contact Groups

Managing contact groups in Outlook allows you to efficiently organize and communicate with multiple contacts simultaneously. This feature is especially useful for sending emails to teams, departments, or any group of people with whom you frequently communicate. Here, we will explore how to manage contact groups, including viewing and editing group details, adding or removing members, and utilizing groups for streamlined communication.

Viewing and Editing Group Details

Once you have created a contact group, it is essential to understand how to view and edit the group's details. This ensures that your contact groups remain up-to-date and relevant.

1. Accessing Contact Groups:

   - Open Outlook and navigate to the "People" or "Contacts" section.

   - Locate the contact group you want to manage. You can search for the group using the search bar or browse through your list of contacts.

   - Double-click on the contact group to open it.

2. Viewing Group Details:

   - When you open a contact group, you will see a list of all the members included in the group.

   - The group details also display the group name, which you can edit if needed.

- Additionally, you can see any notes or additional information that you have added to the group.

3. Editing Group Information:

  - To edit the group's details, click on the "Edit" button.

  - You can change the group name by typing a new name in the "Name" field.

  - Update any notes or additional information in the respective fields.

  - After making the necessary changes, click "Save & Close" to apply the updates.

Adding and Removing Members

Keeping the membership of your contact groups current is vital for effective communication. Outlook makes it easy to add new members or remove existing ones from a contact group.

1. Adding Members:

  - Open the contact group you want to update.

  - Click on the "Add Members" button, usually found in the "Contact Group" tab.

  - You will see several options for adding members:

    - From Outlook Contacts: Select this option to add members from your existing contacts. A dialog box will appear where you can select one or multiple contacts to add to the group.

    - From Address Book: Use this option to add members from your organization's address book.

    - New E-mail Contact: This option allows you to add a member who is not currently in your contacts. You can enter the email address and name of the new member.

  - After selecting or entering the new members, click "OK" to add them to the group.

  - Save the updated group by clicking "Save & Close."

2. Removing Members:

  - Open the contact group from which you want to remove members.

- In the list of group members, select the contact you want to remove. You can select multiple contacts by holding down the "Ctrl" key while clicking on the names.

- Click the "Remove Member" button, usually found in the "Contact Group" tab.

- Confirm the removal if prompted.

- Save the changes by clicking "Save & Close."

Utilizing Contact Groups for Communication

Once you have your contact groups set up and managed, you can use them to streamline your communication processes. Here's how you can efficiently use contact groups in Outlook:

1. Sending Emails to Contact Groups:

  - Open a new email message in Outlook.

  - In the "To" field, start typing the name of the contact group. Outlook will suggest matches from your contacts.

  - Select the contact group from the suggestions.

  - Compose your email as usual and click "Send." The email will be sent to all members of the contact group.

2. Scheduling Meetings with Contact Groups:

  - Open the calendar section in Outlook and create a new meeting.

  - In the "To" field, enter the name of the contact group.

  - Fill in the meeting details, such as the date, time, and location.

  - Click "Send" to schedule the meeting. All members of the contact group will receive an invitation.

3. Using Contact Groups in Tasks:

  - If you use Outlook's task feature, you can assign tasks to contact groups.

  - Open the task you want to assign.

  - In the "Assign Task" tab, enter the name of the contact group in the "To" field.

- Click "Send" to assign the task. All group members will be notified of the task assignment.

Best Practices for Managing Contact Groups

To ensure that your contact groups remain effective and organized, consider the following best practices:

1. Regularly Update Group Membership:

   - Periodically review the members of your contact groups to ensure they are current. Remove any members who no longer need to be part of the group and add new members as necessary.

2. Use Descriptive Group Names:

   - Choose clear and descriptive names for your contact groups. This makes it easier to identify and select the correct group when composing emails or scheduling meetings.

3. Categorize Contact Groups:

   - If you have many contact groups, consider categorizing them. For example, you can create categories for different departments, projects, or types of communication. This helps you quickly find and manage groups.

4. Document Group Changes:

   - Keep a record of any significant changes to your contact groups, such as adding or removing key members. This documentation can be helpful for tracking the evolution of your groups and ensuring consistency in communication.

5. Utilize Group Notes:

   - Use the notes section within a contact group to add relevant information about the group. This can include the group's purpose, important dates, or any other details that may be useful for managing the group.

6. Leverage Contact Group Features:

   - Take advantage of all the features Outlook offers for contact groups. This includes using groups for email, meetings, and tasks, as well as exploring any integrations with other tools you may use.

By following these best practices and effectively managing your contact groups, you can enhance your communication efficiency and ensure that you are always in touch with the right people at the right time.

4.3 Importing and Exporting Contacts

4.3.1 Importing Contacts

Importing contacts into Outlook can save a significant amount of time, especially if you are migrating from another email service or setting up a new Outlook account. This process involves transferring your existing contact list into Outlook, which allows you to maintain continuity and ensure that all important contact information is readily accessible. Below are the detailed steps for importing contacts into Outlook.

Step-by-Step Guide to Importing Contacts

Step 1: Prepare Your Contacts for Importing

Before you start the import process, ensure your contacts are in a format that Outlook can recognize. The most commonly used format for this purpose is a CSV (Comma Separated Values) file. If your contacts are in another format, you may need to convert them to CSV first.

1. Export Contacts from Your Current Service: If you're transferring contacts from another email service (like Gmail, Yahoo Mail, etc.), you'll need to export your contacts from that service. Most email services provide an option to export contacts to a CSV file.

   - In Gmail, for example, you can go to Contacts, select the contacts you want to export, click on "More," then "Export," and choose the CSV format.

   - Save the CSV file to a location on your computer where you can easily find it.

Step 2: Open Outlook

Launch Microsoft Outlook on your computer. Ensure that you are signed in with the account to which you want to import the contacts.

Step 3: Access the Import/Export Wizard

1. Navigate to the File Menu: Click on the "File" tab located in the upper-left corner of the Outlook window. This will open the Backstage view.

2. Select Open & Export: In the sidebar on the left, click on "Open & Export."

3. Choose Import/Export: Click on the "Import/Export" button. This will open the Import and Export Wizard.

Step 4: Choose the Import Option

1. Select "Import from another program or file": In the Import and Export Wizard, select the option "Import from another program or file" and click "Next."

2. Choose the File Type: On the next screen, choose "Comma Separated Values" and click "Next."

Step 5: Locate Your CSV File

1. Browse for Your File: Click on the "Browse" button and navigate to the location where you saved your CSV file. Select the file and click "Open."

2. Handle Duplicates: Choose how you want Outlook to handle duplicate contacts. You have three options:

  - "Replace duplicates with items imported"

  - "Allow duplicates to be created"

  - "Do not import duplicate items"

  Choose the option that best suits your needs and click "Next."

Step 6: Select the Destination Folder

1. Choose Contacts Folder: You will be asked to select a destination folder for your imported contacts. By default, Outlook will choose your main Contacts folder. Ensure that the correct folder is selected and click "Next."

Step 7: Map Custom Fields (if necessary)

1. Map Custom Fields: If your CSV file contains columns that don't match Outlook's default fields, you'll need to map these custom fields. Click on the "Map Custom Fields" button.

  - In the "From" column, you'll see the column names from your CSV file.

  - In the "To" column, you'll see the Outlook fields.

  - Drag and drop each item from the "From" column to the appropriate field in the "To" column.

2. Complete Mapping: Once all fields are correctly mapped, click "OK" to return to the Import and Export Wizard.

Step 8: Complete the Import

1. Start the Import: Click "Finish" to begin importing your contacts into Outlook. The time it takes to complete the import will depend on the number of contacts and the size of the file.

2. Verify Imported Contacts: Once the import is complete, navigate to your Contacts folder in Outlook to verify that your contacts have been successfully imported. Check a few contacts to ensure that all information has been correctly imported.

Common Issues and Troubleshooting

Issue 1: Incorrect CSV File Format

- If you encounter errors during the import process, it may be due to an incorrect CSV file format. Ensure that your CSV file adheres to the correct format and that all necessary columns are present.

Issue 2: Duplicate Contacts

- If you notice duplicate contacts after the import, you can merge or delete them manually. To avoid duplicates in the future, choose the appropriate option in the Import and Export Wizard.

Issue 3: Missing Data

- If some fields are not imported correctly, revisit the "Map Custom Fields" step to ensure all fields are accurately mapped.

Issue 4: Large CSV Files

- For very large CSV files, the import process may take longer or even timeout. Consider breaking the file into smaller parts and importing them separately.

Tips for a Smooth Import Process

1. Backup Your Contacts: Before importing contacts, it's always a good idea to back up your current Outlook contacts. This ensures that you can revert to the original state if something goes wrong during the import.

2. Clean Your Data: Review and clean your contact list before importing. Remove any duplicates or outdated contacts to ensure a streamlined import process.

3. Use a Template: If you're creating a CSV file from scratch, use an Outlook CSV template. This ensures that all required fields are correctly formatted and named.

4. Check Permissions: Ensure you have the necessary permissions to import contacts into the Outlook account you're using, especially if it's a corporate account.

Conclusion

Importing contacts into Outlook is a straightforward process that can significantly enhance your productivity and ensure that all your important contacts are in one place. By following the detailed steps outlined above, you can successfully import your contacts with minimal hassle. Remember to prepare your CSV file correctly, follow each step carefully, and verify your contacts after the import. With your contacts imported into Outlook, you can take full advantage of Outlook's powerful contact management features, making your email communication more efficient and organized.

4.3.2 Exporting Contacts

Exporting contacts from Outlook allows you to create a backup of your contact list or share it with others easily. Whether you need to migrate contacts to another email service or simply want to keep a secure copy, Outlook provides straightforward methods for exporting your contacts.

1. Understanding Export Formats

Outlook supports various export formats to cater to different needs. The common formats include:

- CSV (Comma Separated Values): A widely compatible format suitable for transferring data between different applications. It stores contact information in a plain text format with each field separated by commas.

- PST (Personal Storage Table): This format is specific to Outlook and stores contacts along with other Outlook data such as emails, calendar entries, and tasks. It's useful for creating comprehensive backups of your entire Outlook data.

- Excel Spreadsheet: Exporting contacts to an Excel file (.xlsx) allows for easy viewing and manipulation of contact data using spreadsheet software.

2. Exporting Contacts to CSV Format

Exporting contacts to a CSV file is a versatile option because CSV files can be imported into various applications and services. Here's how to do it:

  - Open Outlook and navigate to the Contacts section.

  - Select the contacts you want to export. You can choose individual contacts or entire contact folders.

  - Go to the "File" menu and click on "Open & Export" > "Import/Export".

  - In the Import and Export Wizard, choose "Export to a file" and then click "Next".

  - Select "Comma Separated Values" as the export format and click "Next".

  - Choose the folder containing the contacts you want to export (e.g., Contacts) and click "Next".

  - Browse to the location where you want to save the exported file, enter a name for the file, and click "Finish".

Outlook will export the selected contacts to a CSV file, which you can then use for backup, transfer, or import into other applications.

3. Exporting Contacts to PST Format

Exporting contacts to a PST file is ideal if you want to create a complete backup of your Outlook data, including contacts. Here's how to export contacts to a PST file:

- Open Outlook and go to the Contacts section.

- Click on "File" > "Open & Export" > "Import/Export".

- Select "Export to a file" and then click "Next".

- Choose "Outlook Data File (.pst)" as the export format and click "Next".

- Select the folder containing the contacts you want to export (e.g., Contacts) and click "Next".

- Browse to the location where you want to save the PST file, enter a name for the file, and click "Finish".

Outlook will export the selected contacts along with other data in the chosen folder to a PST file, preserving the hierarchical structure and metadata.

4. Exporting Contacts to an Excel Spreadsheet

If you prefer to work with contact data in a spreadsheet format, you can export contacts to an Excel file (.xlsx). Here's how to do it:

- Open Outlook and navigate to the Contacts section.

- Select the contacts you want to export.

- Go to "File" > "Open & Export" > "Import/Export".

- Choose "Export to a file" and then click "Next".

- Select "Microsoft Excel" as the export format and click "Next".

- Choose the folder containing the contacts you want to export (e.g., Contacts) and click "Next".

- Browse to the location where you want to save the Excel file, enter a name for the file, and click "Finish".

Outlook will export the selected contacts to an Excel spreadsheet (.xlsx), where you can view, edit, and analyze contact information using Excel's features.

5. Tips for Successful Contact Export

- Verify Exported Data: After exporting contacts, open the exported file in the respective application (e.g., Excel for .xlsx files) to ensure that all contact details are correctly exported.

- Regular Backups: Schedule regular exports of your contacts to maintain up-to-date backups, ensuring you have a secure copy of your contacts in case of data loss or device failure.

- Security Considerations: When handling exported contact files, store them in secure locations and be cautious when sharing them, especially if they contain sensitive information.

By mastering the export options in Outlook, you can efficiently manage and safeguard your contact information, ensuring accessibility and security across different platforms and applications.

CHAPTER V
Calendar and Scheduling

5.1 Introduction to the Calendar

The calendar in Microsoft Outlook is a powerful tool designed to help you manage your time efficiently. It allows you to schedule appointments, set reminders, organize meetings, and keep track of your tasks, all in one place. Whether you're a busy professional juggling multiple meetings a day or someone who simply wants to keep track of personal appointments, the Outlook calendar provides a range of features to meet your needs.

The calendar interface is user-friendly and integrates seamlessly with your email and other Outlook functionalities. This integration ensures that all your events, appointments, and meetings are synchronized across your devices, keeping you up-to-date and organized. In this section, we will explore the various aspects of the Outlook calendar, starting with an overview of the different calendar views.

5.1.1 Calendar Views

Outlook offers several calendar views to help you visualize your schedule in the way that best suits your needs. Each view presents your calendar information differently, allowing you to focus on specific time frames or types of activities. The main calendar views in Outlook include:

1. Day View

2. Work Week View

3. Week View

4. Month View

5. Schedule View

Day View

The Day View is designed for those who need to focus on the details of a single day. It displays all your appointments, meetings, and events in a chronological order, giving you a clear picture of what your day looks like. This view is particularly useful for busy professionals who have multiple engagements in a day. You can see the start and end times of each event, as well as any overlapping appointments.

- Navigating the Day View: You can move between days using the arrow buttons at the top of the calendar. The current day is highlighted, making it easy to identify. You can also use the date picker on the left to jump to a specific date.

- Customization Options: The Day View can be customized to show more or fewer hours in a day. You can also adjust the time intervals, such as displaying your schedule in 15-minute or 30-minute increments.

Work Week View

The Work Week View focuses on the days you typically work, usually Monday through Friday. This view is ideal for professionals who want to concentrate on their work-related activities without the distraction of weekends. It provides a broader perspective than the Day View but still maintains a detailed look at each day.

- Navigating the Work Week View: Similar to the Day View, you can navigate between weeks using the arrow buttons. The date picker can also be used to jump to a specific week.

- Customization Options: You can define your work week settings in Outlook's calendar options. For example, you can set which days constitute your work week and the start and end times for your workday.

Week View

The Week View displays all seven days of the week, providing a comprehensive overview of your schedule. This view is useful for planning ahead and balancing work and personal commitments. You can see all your appointments, meetings, and events for the entire week, making it easier to manage your time.

- Navigating the Week View: Use the arrow buttons to move between weeks or the date picker to select a specific week. The current week is typically highlighted.

- Customization Options: You can adjust the start day of the week and the time intervals displayed. This allows you to tailor the view to your preferences.

Month View

The Month View offers a bird's-eye view of your schedule for the entire month. It is perfect for long-term planning and seeing how your time is distributed over weeks. This view shows your appointments, meetings, and events in a compact format, with each day represented as a small box.

- Navigating the Month View: You can scroll through months using the arrow buttons or select a specific month using the date picker. The current month is highlighted for easy identification.

- Customization Options: The Month View can be customized to show different levels of detail. For example, you can choose to display only the most important events or all events for each day.

Schedule View

The Schedule View is designed for managing multiple calendars simultaneously. It arranges your calendar in a timeline format, making it easy to see overlapping appointments and meetings. This view is particularly useful for team collaboration, allowing you to see the schedules of your colleagues alongside your own.

- Navigating the Schedule View: You can navigate through the timeline using the scroll bar. The current date and time are highlighted for quick reference.

- Customization Options: You can add or remove calendars from the Schedule View, allowing you to focus on the most relevant schedules. You can also adjust the time scale to show more or less detail.

Customizing Calendar Views

Outlook allows you to customize each calendar view to better suit your needs. Here are some common customization options available across all views:

- Changing Time Intervals: You can change the time intervals displayed in your calendar. For example, you might prefer to see your day broken down into 15-minute intervals instead of 30-minute intervals.

- Color Coding: Outlook allows you to color-code your appointments and events. This helps you quickly distinguish between different types of activities, such as work meetings, personal appointments, and reminders.

- Adding Calendars: You can add multiple calendars to your Outlook account. This is useful if you want to manage separate calendars for work, personal life, and other activities. You can view these calendars side-by-side or overlay them to see all your commitments in one place.

- Changing Calendar Settings: In the calendar settings, you can adjust various options such as the default reminder times, working hours, and the first day of the week. These settings help tailor the calendar to your personal preferences and working style.

Syncing Your Calendar

One of the key benefits of using Outlook is the ability to sync your calendar across multiple devices. This ensures that your schedule is always up-to-date, whether you're using your desktop computer, laptop, tablet, or smartphone. Outlook can sync with various services, including:

- Exchange Server: If you use Outlook as part of a corporate email system, it is likely connected to an Exchange server. This allows for seamless syncing of emails, contacts, and calendars across all your devices.

- Outlook.com: If you use an Outlook.com account, your calendar can sync with the Outlook app on your mobile devices. This ensures that any changes you make to your calendar on one device are reflected on all your devices.

- Third-Party Calendars: Outlook can also sync with third-party calendar services, such as Google Calendar and Apple Calendar. This allows you to consolidate your schedule from different sources into one place.

Using Calendar Reminders

Reminders are an essential feature of the Outlook calendar, helping you stay on top of your appointments and tasks. You can set reminders for any event in your calendar, ensuring that you never miss an important meeting or deadline. Reminders can be customized to appear at specific times before an event, giving you plenty of notice to prepare.

- Setting Reminders: When creating an appointment or event, you can set a reminder to appear a few minutes, hours, or even days before the scheduled time. You can choose from predefined reminder times or set a custom reminder.

- Managing Reminders: Reminders appear as pop-up notifications on your screen. You can snooze a reminder if you need more time or dismiss it if you're ready to take action. In the calendar settings, you can also configure how reminders are displayed and managed across your devices.

By understanding and utilizing these calendar views and customization options, you can optimize your schedule management in Outlook. Each view offers unique advantages, and by switching between them as needed, you can gain better control over your time and commitments.

5.1.2 Navigating the Calendar

Navigating the calendar in Outlook is a fundamental skill that enables users to efficiently manage their schedules, plan meetings, and stay on top of important appointments. This section will provide a detailed overview of how to navigate the calendar interface, utilize various views, and make the most of the calendar's features to enhance productivity.

Understanding the Calendar Interface

The Outlook calendar interface is designed to be intuitive and user-friendly, offering multiple ways to view and manage your schedule. Here are the key components of the calendar interface:

1. Navigation Pane: Located on the left side of the Outlook window, the Navigation Pane allows you to switch between different modules, such as Mail, Calendar, People, and Tasks. When you select the Calendar module, the Navigation Pane will display a small monthly calendar, which can be used to quickly jump to specific dates.

2. Ribbon: The Ribbon is located at the top of the Outlook window and contains various tabs and commands specific to the Calendar module. Tabs like "Home," "Send/Receive," "Folder," and "View" provide quick access to commonly used calendar functions.

3. Calendar View Area: This is the main area where your calendar entries are displayed. Depending on the selected view, you can see your schedule for the day, week, or month.

4. Reading Pane: When you select a calendar item, such as an appointment or meeting, the details of that item are displayed in the Reading Pane. This allows you to quickly review information without opening a new window.

5. To-Do Bar: The To-Do Bar, usually located on the right side of the Outlook window, shows a summary of upcoming appointments, tasks, and flagged emails. It helps you stay organized by providing a snapshot of your schedule and priorities.

Navigating Calendar Views

Outlook offers several calendar views to help you manage your time effectively. Each view serves a different purpose and provides unique insights into your schedule.

1. Day View: The Day View shows a detailed breakdown of your schedule for a single day. It includes time slots, making it easy to see how your day is allocated. This view is ideal for managing daily appointments and tasks.

2. Work Week View: The Work Week View displays your schedule for the workweek, typically Monday through Friday. This view is useful for planning your work commitments and ensuring you have balanced workloads throughout the week.

3. Week View: The Week View shows your schedule for the entire week, including weekends. It provides a broader perspective on your activities and is helpful for planning both work and personal events.

4. Month View: The Month View offers a high-level overview of your schedule for the entire month. It displays appointments and meetings as blocks, allowing you to see how your time is distributed over several weeks.

5. Schedule View: The Schedule View, also known as the Timeline View, is designed for viewing the schedules of multiple people or resources side by side. This view is particularly useful for scheduling meetings with several attendees or managing shared resources.

Switching Between Views

Switching between calendar views in Outlook is straightforward and can be done using the following methods:

1. View Tab: Click on the "View" tab in the Ribbon. Here, you will find options to switch between Day, Work Week, Week, and Month views. Simply click on the desired view to switch.

2. Navigation Pane: In the Navigation Pane, you can quickly jump to different views by selecting the appropriate date. For example, clicking on a specific date in the small monthly calendar will switch to the Day View for that date.

3. Keyboard Shortcuts: Outlook supports keyboard shortcuts for quickly switching between views. For example, pressing "Ctrl+Alt+1" will switch to Day View, "Ctrl+Alt+2" to Work Week View, "Ctrl+Alt+3" to Week View, and "Ctrl+Alt+4" to Month View.

Exploring Calendar Options

Outlook provides several options to customize your calendar experience. These options can be accessed through the "View" tab in the Ribbon or by right-clicking on the calendar interface.

1. Change View: The "Change View" option allows you to customize the current view by selecting predefined settings or creating your own. For example, you can choose to display additional details, adjust the time scale, or hide weekends.

2. Color Categories: Color categories help you visually organize your calendar entries. You can assign different colors to appointments, meetings, and tasks to quickly identify them. For example, you might use one color for work-related meetings and another for personal appointments.

3. Overlay Mode: Overlay mode allows you to view multiple calendars simultaneously by overlaying them on top of each other. This is particularly useful if you manage multiple calendars, such as a work calendar and a personal calendar.

4. Split View: Split View enables you to view your calendar alongside another module, such as Mail or Tasks. This allows you to manage your schedule while keeping an eye on your inbox or task list.

5. Time Zones: If you work with people in different time zones, you can add additional time zones to your calendar. This feature helps you schedule meetings and appointments across different regions without confusion.

Creating and Managing Calendar Entries

Navigating the calendar also involves creating and managing various types of calendar entries, such as appointments, meetings, and all-day events. Here are the basic steps:

1. Creating Appointments: To create an appointment, click on the "New Appointment" button in the "Home" tab or double-click on the desired time slot in the calendar. Fill in the necessary details, such as the subject, location, start and end times, and any additional notes. Click "Save & Close" to add the appointment to your calendar.

2. Scheduling Meetings: To schedule a meeting, click on the "New Meeting" button in the "Home" tab. Enter the meeting details, including the subject, location, start and end times, and any required attendees. You can also use the Scheduling Assistant to find a suitable time for all participants. Click "Send" to send the meeting request.

3. Creating All-Day Events: All-day events are useful for marking full-day activities, such as holidays, birthdays, or conferences. To create an all-day event, click on the "New Appointment" button, enter the event details, and select the "All day event" checkbox. Click "Save & Close" to add the event to your calendar.

4. Recurring Entries: Many appointments and meetings occur on a regular basis. To create a recurring entry, open the appointment or meeting window and click on the "Recurrence" button. Choose the recurrence pattern (daily, weekly, monthly, or yearly), specify the recurrence range, and click "OK." Click "Save & Close" to save the recurring entry.

Navigating and Managing Calendar Entries

Once you have created calendar entries, it's important to know how to navigate and manage them effectively:

1. Viewing Entry Details: To view the details of a calendar entry, simply click on it. The Reading Pane will display the entry's details, including the subject, location, attendees, and any notes. You can also double-click the entry to open it in a separate window for more detailed viewing and editing.

2. Editing Entries: To edit a calendar entry, double-click on it to open it in a new window. Make the necessary changes and click "Save & Close" to update the entry. For recurring entries, you can choose to edit a single occurrence or the entire series.

3. Deleting Entries: To delete a calendar entry, select it and press the "Delete" key on your keyboard, or right-click the entry and choose "Delete" from the context menu. For recurring entries, you can choose to delete a single occurrence or the entire series.

4. Moving Entries: To move a calendar entry to a different time slot or date, click and drag the entry to the desired location. You can also use the "Cut" and "Paste" commands in the context menu to move entries.

5. Copying Entries: To create a copy of a calendar entry, right-click on it and choose "Copy." Then, right-click on the desired time slot or date and choose "Paste." This is useful for duplicating appointments or meetings with similar details.

6. Responding to Meeting Invitations: When you receive a meeting invitation, it will appear in your inbox. Open the invitation to view the details and choose your response: "Accept," "Tentative," "Decline," or "Propose New Time." Your response will be sent to the meeting organizer, and the meeting will be added to your calendar accordingly.

Conclusion

Navigating the Outlook calendar is an essential skill for managing your time effectively. By understanding the calendar interface, utilizing various views, and making the most of calendar options, you can streamline your schedule and enhance your productivity. Whether you are creating appointments, scheduling meetings, or managing recurring events, mastering calendar navigation in Outlook will help you stay organized and on top of your commitments.

CHAPTER V: ADVANCED ANALYTICS WITH DAX

5.2 Creating and Managing Appointments

Creating and managing appointments in Outlook is a fundamental skill that can significantly enhance your productivity. This section will guide you through the process of adding, editing, and organizing your appointments in Outlook. By mastering these features, you can ensure that you never miss an important meeting or event.

5.2.1 Adding Appointments

Adding appointments in Outlook is a straightforward process, but understanding the various options and settings available can help you make the most of this feature. Here's a detailed guide to help you add appointments efficiently:

Step-by-Step Guide to Adding Appointments

1. Open Outlook Calendar:

   - Launch Outlook and navigate to the Calendar by clicking on the calendar icon in the lower-left corner of the Outlook window. This will open the Calendar view.

2. Create a New Appointment:

   - There are several ways to create a new appointment:

     - Click on the "New Appointment" button in the Home tab.

     - Right-click on the desired time slot in your calendar and select "New Appointment."

     - Double-click on the desired time slot in your calendar.

3. Enter Appointment Details:

   - In the appointment window, enter the following details:

     - Subject: This is the title of your appointment. Make it descriptive and concise.

     - Location: Specify where the appointment will take place. This can be a physical location or a virtual meeting link.

- Start and End Time: Choose the date and time for the appointment. You can also set the appointment to be an all-day event by checking the "All day event" box.

- Reminder: Set a reminder for the appointment. This will notify you a specified time before the appointment starts. The default reminder is usually 15 minutes before the start time, but you can adjust this as needed.

4. Add Recurrence (if applicable):

- If the appointment is recurring, click on the "Recurrence" button in the Options group. This opens the Appointment Recurrence dialog box, where you can set the pattern for the recurrence (daily, weekly, monthly, or yearly) and specify the range of recurrence (start and end dates).

5. Add Details in the Body:

- Use the body of the appointment to add any additional information or notes related to the appointment. This can include an agenda, important points to discuss, or any preparatory material.

6. Set Categories and Sensitivity (optional):

- You can categorize your appointment by clicking on the "Categorize" button in the Tags group and selecting a category. This helps in organizing and color-coding your appointments.

- Set the sensitivity of the appointment (Normal, Personal, Private, or Confidential) by clicking on the "Private" button in the Tags group if you want to restrict visibility to other users.

7. Save and Close:

- Once you have entered all the necessary information, click on the "Save & Close" button in the Actions group to save the appointment to your calendar.

Advanced Options for Adding Appointments

- Using Quick Steps:

- Quick Steps in Outlook allows you to automate common tasks. You can create a Quick Step to streamline the process of adding appointments by predefining certain fields. This is particularly useful for recurring types of appointments.

- Drag and Drop:

 - You can also create an appointment by dragging an email to the calendar icon. This automatically opens a new appointment window with the email content copied into the body. You can then edit the details as needed.

- Using Templates:

 - If you frequently create similar appointments, consider creating appointment templates. To do this, create an appointment with all the standard details and save it as an Outlook Template (.oft) file. You can then use this template to quickly create new appointments with the same settings.

Best Practices for Adding Appointments

- Be Specific and Clear:

 - Ensure that the subject and location fields are clear and specific. This helps in quickly identifying the purpose and place of the appointment at a glance.

- Use Categories:

 - Categorize your appointments to organize them effectively. Use color coding to differentiate between personal, professional, and other types of appointments.

- Set Appropriate Reminders:

 - Set reminders that give you enough time to prepare for the appointment. Adjust the default reminder time to suit your needs for different types of appointments.

- Include Necessary Details:

 - Use the body of the appointment to include any necessary details or attachments. This ensures that all the relevant information is in one place.

Troubleshooting Common Issues

- Appointment Not Showing in Calendar:

 - If an appointment does not appear in your calendar, ensure that you have saved it correctly. Check if you are viewing the correct calendar if you have multiple calendars.

- Reminder Not Working:

 - If reminders are not working, check your reminder settings in Outlook options. Ensure that the reminder option is enabled and that the sound is not muted.

- Recurring Appointment Conflicts:

 - If a recurring appointment conflicts with other events, review the recurrence pattern and adjust it as needed. Consider setting exceptions for specific instances of the recurrence.

Conclusion

Adding appointments in Outlook is a fundamental skill that, when mastered, can significantly enhance your time management and productivity. By following the steps outlined in this guide and utilizing the advanced options and best practices, you can efficiently manage your schedule and ensure that you never miss an important event. Whether you are using Outlook for personal, professional, or academic purposes, understanding how to create and manage appointments is essential for staying organized and on top of your commitments.

5.2.2 Recurring Appointments

Recurring appointments in Outlook are useful for events or meetings that happen regularly, such as weekly team meetings, monthly project reviews, or annual reminders. By setting up a recurring appointment, you save time and ensure that the event is consistently scheduled without the need to create a new appointment for each occurrence. In this section, we'll walk through the steps for creating, managing, and customizing recurring appointments in Outlook.

Creating a Recurring Appointment

1. Open Outlook Calendar: Start by opening Outlook and navigating to the Calendar view. You can do this by clicking on the "Calendar" icon in the navigation pane.

2. Create a New Appointment: Click on "New Appointment" in the Home tab. This opens a new appointment window.

3. Enter Appointment Details: Fill in the necessary details for your appointment:

  - Subject: Enter a descriptive title for your appointment.

  - Location: Specify the location where the appointment will take place.

  - Start and End Time: Set the start and end times for the first occurrence of the appointment.

4. Set Recurrence: Click on the "Recurrence" button in the ribbon to open the Appointment Recurrence dialog box. Here, you can define the recurrence pattern for your appointment.

5. Define Recurrence Pattern: In the Appointment Recurrence dialog box, specify the recurrence pattern:

  - Recurrence Pattern Options: Choose whether the appointment recurs daily, weekly, monthly, or yearly.

    - Daily: Set the appointment to occur every specified number of days.

    - Weekly: Choose the days of the week and the interval (e.g., every 1 week).

    - Monthly: Set the appointment to recur on a specific day of the month or a specific day of the week within the month.

    - Yearly: Set the appointment to recur on a specific date each year.

  - Range of Recurrence: Define the start date and either set an end date or specify the number of occurrences. If you choose "No end date," the appointment will continue indefinitely.

6. Save the Recurrence: Once you have configured the recurrence pattern, click "OK" to save the recurrence settings and return to the appointment window.

7. Save the Appointment: Click "Save & Close" to create the recurring appointment in your calendar. You will now see the appointment repeated according to the recurrence pattern you specified.

Managing Recurring Appointments

Once you have created a recurring appointment, you may need to make adjustments to individual occurrences or the entire series. Outlook provides flexibility in managing recurring appointments, allowing you to edit, move, or delete them as needed.

1. Edit a Single Occurrence: To edit a single occurrence of a recurring appointment:

   - Open the Occurrence: Double-click on the occurrence you want to edit. Outlook will prompt you to choose whether you want to open just this occurrence or the entire series. Select "Just this one" and click "OK."

   - Make Changes: Modify the appointment details as needed. You can change the subject, location, time, or any other details specific to this occurrence.

   - Save Changes: Click "Save & Close" to apply the changes to this single occurrence.

2. Edit the Entire Series: To edit all occurrences of a recurring appointment:

   - Open the Series: Double-click on any occurrence of the recurring appointment. When prompted, select "The entire series" and click "OK."

   - Make Changes: Modify the details in the appointment window. Changes made here will apply to all occurrences in the series.

   - Save Changes: Click "Save & Close" to update the entire series.

3. Move a Single Occurrence: If you need to move a single occurrence to a different date or time:

   - Drag and Drop: In the calendar view, click and drag the occurrence to the new date or time slot. Release the mouse button to drop the appointment in the new location.

   - Edit Details: Alternatively, you can double-click the occurrence, select "Just this one," and manually update the start and end times. Click "Save & Close" to apply the changes.

4. Move the Entire Series: To move the entire series to a new time slot:

   - Open the Series: Double-click any occurrence and select "The entire series."

   - Update Times: Change the start and end times in the appointment window. Click "Save & Close" to move the entire series to the new time slot.

5. Delete a Single Occurrence: To delete a single occurrence of a recurring appointment:

   - Open the Occurrence: Double-click on the occurrence you want to delete and select "Just this one."

- Delete: Click the "Delete" button in the ribbon. This will remove the selected occurrence from your calendar.

6. Delete the Entire Series: To delete all occurrences of a recurring appointment:

  - Open the Series: Double-click any occurrence and select "The entire series."

  - Delete: Click the "Delete" button in the ribbon. This will remove the entire series from your calendar.

Customizing Recurrence Patterns

Outlook offers several options to customize the recurrence patterns of your appointments, allowing you to tailor them to fit your specific needs.

1. Custom Daily Recurrence: Instead of a fixed daily pattern, you can set custom intervals (e.g., every 2 days, every weekday).

2. Custom Weekly Recurrence: Specify the days of the week the appointment should occur (e.g., every Monday, Wednesday, and Friday).

3. Custom Monthly Recurrence: Choose specific days or a combination of day and week (e.g., the third Tuesday of every month).

4. Custom Yearly Recurrence: Set the appointment to recur on a specific date or a combination of month and day (e.g., the first Monday of June every year).

5. End Recurrence After a Number of Occurrences: If the appointment is only relevant for a specific number of occurrences, you can set it to end after that number (e.g., end after 10 occurrences).

6. Using Exceptions: You can add exceptions to your recurring appointments, such as holidays or specific dates when the appointment should not occur:

  - Add Exceptions: Open the series and navigate to the "Recurrence" dialog. Use the "Add Exception" feature to specify dates to exclude.

  - Remove Exceptions: If you need to remove an exception, open the recurrence pattern and delete the specified exception date.

Best Practices for Recurring Appointments

To effectively manage your recurring appointments and avoid potential conflicts or confusion, consider the following best practices:

1. Clear and Descriptive Titles: Use clear and descriptive titles for your recurring appointments to easily identify them in your calendar.

2. Consistent Time Slots: Schedule recurring appointments in consistent time slots to create a predictable and organized schedule.

3. Regular Review and Updates: Periodically review your recurring appointments to ensure they are still relevant and make necessary updates.

4. Avoid Overlapping Appointments: Be mindful of potential overlaps with other appointments or meetings to avoid scheduling conflicts.

5. Communicate Changes: If the recurring appointment involves other participants, communicate any changes in schedule or details promptly.

By following these steps and best practices, you can effectively create, manage, and customize recurring appointments in Outlook, ensuring that your schedule remains organized and efficient. Recurring appointments are a powerful feature that, when used correctly, can greatly enhance your productivity and help you stay on top of your commitments.

5.3 Scheduling Meetings

Scheduling meetings in Outlook is a powerful feature that helps you efficiently manage your time and collaborate with others. With Outlook, you can easily set up meeting requests, invite participants, and track responses. This section will guide you through the process of creating a meeting request in Outlook, ensuring you make the most of its robust scheduling capabilities.

5.3.1 Creating a Meeting Request

Creating a meeting request in Outlook involves several straightforward steps. Whether you're scheduling a simple one-on-one meeting or coordinating a large group meeting, Outlook provides all the tools you need. Here's a step-by-step guide to help you create a meeting request.

Step 1: Open the Calendar

1. Navigate to the Calendar: To start, open Outlook and navigate to the Calendar view. You can do this by clicking on the calendar icon located in the bottom-left corner of the Outlook window.

2. Choose a Date and Time: Select the date and time slot for your meeting. You can do this by either clicking on the specific time slot in the day view or by selecting a range of time in the week or month view.

Step 2: Create a New Meeting Request

1. New Meeting: Click on the "New Meeting" button located in the Home tab of the Calendar. Alternatively, you can right-click on the selected time slot and choose "New Meeting Request" from the context menu.

2. Meeting Form: This will open the Meeting form, where you can fill in the details of your meeting.

Step 3: Enter Meeting Details

1. Title: In the "Subject" field, enter a concise title for your meeting. This should clearly describe the purpose of the meeting.

2. Location: In the "Location" field, enter the location of the meeting. This could be a physical location, such as a conference room, or a virtual location, such as a video conferencing link. Outlook can also integrate with room booking systems if set up by your organization.

3. Start and End Times: Specify the start and end times for your meeting. You can manually enter the times or use the drop-down menus to select them. Ensure the times are convenient for all participants.

Step 4: Invite Attendees

1. To Field: In the "To" field, enter the email addresses of the people you want to invite to the meeting. You can type them manually or select them from your contacts by clicking the "To" button, which will open the Address Book.

2. Optional Attendees: If there are people who are not essential to the meeting but whom you would like to keep informed, you can add them as optional attendees. Click on the "Optional" button next to the "To" field and add their email addresses.

3. Required vs. Optional Attendees: Clearly distinguish between required and optional attendees to set the right expectations. Required attendees are crucial for the meeting's objectives, while optional attendees are informed but not necessary for decision-making.

Step 5: Set the Meeting Options

1. Recurring Meetings: If your meeting is going to occur on a regular basis, you can set it as a recurring meeting. Click on the "Recurrence" button in the Meeting form, and choose the frequency (daily, weekly, monthly, etc.), start and end dates, and other recurrence options. This is particularly useful for weekly team meetings or monthly status updates.

2. Reminder: Set a reminder for your meeting. By default, Outlook sets a reminder for 15 minutes before the meeting. You can adjust this to any time that suits your needs. Reminders help ensure that you and your attendees are notified in advance of the meeting.

Step 6: Add Meeting Agenda and Notes

1. Agenda: In the body of the Meeting form, you can add the meeting agenda. This helps attendees understand the purpose of the meeting and prepare accordingly. A well-structured agenda includes the main topics to be discussed, the order of discussion, and the time allocated for each topic.

2. Attachments: If there are any documents, presentations, or other files that attendees need to review before or during the meeting, you can attach them to the meeting request. Click on the "Insert" tab and choose "Attach File" to add attachments. This ensures everyone has access to the necessary materials in advance.

Step 7: Check Scheduling Conflicts

1. Scheduling Assistant: To avoid conflicts with other meetings or appointments, use the Scheduling Assistant. Click on the "Scheduling Assistant" button in the Meeting form. This tool shows the availability of all attendees and suggests the best times for the meeting based on their schedules.

2. Suggested Times: Outlook may suggest alternative times if there are conflicts. Consider adjusting the meeting time based on these suggestions to accommodate as many attendees as possible.

Step 8: Send the Meeting Request

1. Review and Send: Once all details are filled out and you've checked for scheduling conflicts, review your meeting request to ensure everything is correct. Double-check the date, time, location, attendees, and any attached files.

2. Send: Click on the "Send" button to dispatch the meeting request. Outlook will send invitations to all attendees and add the meeting to your calendar as well as to the calendars of the invitees.

Step 9: Track Responses

1. Tracking Responses: After sending the meeting request, you can track responses from attendees. Open the meeting in your calendar and click on the "Tracking" button. This shows who has accepted, declined, or tentatively accepted the invitation.

2. Follow-up: If necessary, follow up with attendees who have not responded. This ensures you have a clear understanding of who will be attending the meeting and allows you to make any necessary adjustments.

Step 10: Modify or Cancel the Meeting

1. Modifying the Meeting: If you need to change the details of the meeting (e.g., time, location, or attendees), open the meeting in your calendar and make the necessary changes. Click "Send Update" to notify attendees of the changes.

2. Cancelling the Meeting: If the meeting is no longer needed, you can cancel it. Open the meeting in your calendar and click on the "Cancel Meeting" button. Outlook will send a cancellation notice to all attendees and remove the meeting from their calendars.

5.3.2 Managing Meeting Responses

When you schedule a meeting in Outlook, it's crucial to manage the responses effectively to ensure the meeting is productive and well-attended. Managing meeting responses involves tracking who has accepted, declined, or tentatively accepted your meeting invitation, and making necessary adjustments based on these responses. Here's a detailed guide on how to manage meeting responses in Outlook.

Tracking Responses

Once you send out a meeting invitation, Outlook provides tools to help you keep track of attendee responses. Here's how you can do it:

1. Open the Meeting Invitation:

   - Go to your Calendar and find the meeting for which you want to track responses.

   - Double-click on the meeting to open it.

2. View the Tracking Information:

   - In the meeting window, navigate to the "Tracking" tab. This tab shows a list of all the attendees along with their responses: Accepted, Declined, Tentative, or No Response.

   - This allows you to quickly see who has responded and who hasn't.

3. Using the Response Pane:

   - Outlook also displays a response pane on the right side of the meeting window. This pane gives a summary of the responses and highlights any issues, such as conflicts in attendees' schedules.

Handling Responses

Once you have tracked the responses, the next step is to handle them appropriately. Here are some actions you might take:

1. Follow Up with Non-Responders:

  - If some attendees have not responded, you can send them a reminder. To do this, click on the "Message" tab, and select "Reply with Meeting" or "Forward as iCalendar" to resend the invitation.

  - Craft a polite reminder asking them to respond to the invitation.

2. Addressing Declines:

  - If key participants decline the invitation, you may need to reach out to them to understand why they can't attend. Sometimes, rescheduling the meeting might be necessary.

  - You can also look for alternative attendees if the original invitee cannot make it.

3. Managing Tentative Responses:

  - For those who responded tentatively, consider following up to confirm their attendance closer to the meeting date. Tentative responses can often change to a definitive yes or no as the date approaches.

4. Updating the Meeting:

  - Based on the responses, you might need to update the meeting details. This could involve changing the meeting time, adding a new location, or including additional resources.

  - To update the meeting, open the meeting invitation, make the necessary changes, and click "Send Update." This ensures all attendees receive the updated information.

Communicating Changes

When you make changes to a meeting, it's important to communicate these changes clearly to all attendees. Here's how:

1. Send Updates:

  - After making any changes to the meeting, click "Send Update" to notify all attendees of the modifications. This ensures everyone is aware of the new details.

2. Include a Note:

  - When sending the update, include a note explaining the changes. This helps attendees understand what has been modified and why. For example, "Due to a scheduling conflict, the meeting has been moved to 3 PM."

3. Confirm with Key Attendees:

  - For critical meetings, you might want to personally confirm the changes with key attendees. This can be done through a quick email or a phone call.

Using Outlook's Automatic Features

Outlook provides several automatic features to help manage meeting responses more efficiently:

1. Automatic Tracking:

  - Outlook automatically tracks responses and updates the meeting organizer with the status of each invitee. This feature saves time and reduces manual tracking efforts.

2. Meeting Polls:

  - For larger meetings or when trying to find the best time for all attendees, consider using the "Meeting Poll" feature. This allows you to propose multiple time slots and let attendees vote on their preferred time.

  - Once the poll is completed, you can schedule the meeting based on the most popular time slot.

Best Practices for Managing Meeting Responses

1. Set Clear Expectations:

  - In your meeting invitation, set clear expectations regarding the importance of the meeting and the need for timely responses. This can encourage prompt and definitive replies.

2. Provide All Necessary Information:

- Ensure your meeting invitation includes all necessary information, such as the agenda, location, and any preparatory work needed. This helps attendees make an informed decision about their availability.

3. Be Flexible:

  - Be prepared to reschedule or adjust the meeting based on the responses. Flexibility can increase attendance and ensure the meeting's success.

4. Use Outlook's Collaboration Tools:

  - Utilize Outlook's collaboration tools such as shared calendars and scheduling assistants to find the best time for your meeting. This can minimize conflicts and improve response rates.

5. Follow Up:

  - Don't hesitate to follow up with non-responders or those who declined. Understanding their reasons can provide insights and help in planning future meetings more effectively.

Handling Last-Minute Changes

Sometimes, despite your best efforts, last-minute changes or cancellations occur. Here's how to handle them:

1. Last-Minute Cancellations:

  - If key attendees cancel at the last minute, assess the impact on the meeting. You may need to reschedule or proceed with the remaining attendees.

  - Communicate any changes promptly to all participants.

2. Emergency Rescheduling:

  - In case of an emergency rescheduling, use Outlook to quickly find an alternative time. The "Propose New Time" feature allows attendees to suggest new meeting times, making it easier to find a suitable slot.

3. Keep Everyone Informed:

  - Ensure that all changes are communicated clearly and promptly. This helps avoid confusion and ensures everyone is on the same page.

Managing meeting responses in Outlook requires careful tracking, prompt follow-ups, and effective communication. By leveraging Outlook's features and adopting best practices, you can ensure your meetings are well-organized and attended, leading to productive and successful outcomes.

5.4 Using Calendar Reminders

5.4.1 Setting Reminders

Managing your time effectively is crucial in both personal and professional environments, and Outlook's calendar reminders are a powerful tool to help you stay on top of your schedule. Reminders in Outlook are designed to alert you about upcoming appointments, meetings, or tasks, ensuring you never miss an important event. In this section, we will explore how to set reminders for different calendar items, customize reminder settings, and manage your reminders effectively.

What are Calendar Reminders?

Calendar reminders are notifications that alert you to upcoming events on your Outlook calendar. These notifications can appear as pop-ups on your screen, sounds, or even emails, depending on how you have configured your settings. Reminders are particularly useful for managing deadlines, preparing for meetings, and ensuring that you allocate enough time for important tasks.

Setting Reminders for Appointments and Meetings

Outlook allows you to set reminders for both appointments and meetings, helping you prepare in advance. Here's a step-by-step guide on how to set these reminders:

Step 1: Open Your Calendar

To set a reminder, start by opening your Outlook calendar. You can do this by clicking on the calendar icon in the navigation pane on the bottom left of the Outlook window.

Step 2: Create or Open an Appointment or Meeting

If you want to set a reminder for a new appointment or meeting, click on "New Appointment" or "New Meeting" in the Home tab. If you want to add a reminder to an existing event, double-click the event to open it.

Step 3: Set the Reminder

In the appointment or meeting window, look for the "Reminder" dropdown menu. This menu is usually located in the options section of the event window. The default reminder time is typically 15 minutes before the event, but you can change this to any time period you prefer. The dropdown menu offers a range of options, from 0 minutes (at the time of the event) to 2 weeks before the event.

Step 4: Save the Event

Once you have selected the desired reminder time, save the event by clicking "Save & Close" for appointments or "Send" for meetings. Your reminder is now set, and you will receive a notification at the specified time.

Customizing Reminder Settings

Outlook provides various options to customize how you receive reminders, allowing you to tailor the notifications to your preferences.

Changing the Default Reminder Time

If you find that you frequently adjust the reminder time for your events, you may want to change the default reminder time. Here's how you can do it:

1. Go to the "File" tab and select "Options."

2. In the Outlook Options window, click on "Calendar."

3. Under "Calendar options," you will see a field labeled "Default reminders." Use the dropdown menu to select your preferred default reminder time.

4. Click "OK" to save your changes.

Now, every new appointment or meeting will automatically have your chosen default reminder time.

Customizing Reminder Notifications

Outlook allows you to customize the type of notification you receive for reminders. You can choose between visual pop-ups, sound alerts, or email notifications. Here's how you can adjust these settings:

1. Go to the "File" tab and select "Options."

2. In the Outlook Options window, click on "Advanced."

3. Scroll down to the "Reminders" section.

4. To enable or disable sound notifications, check or uncheck the box labeled "Play reminder sound." You can also change the sound by clicking on "Browse" and selecting a different audio file.

5. To enable or disable email reminders, you may need to use third-party add-ins or configure rules within Outlook, as built-in email reminders are limited.

Click "OK" to save your changes.

Setting Reminders for All-Day Events

All-day events, such as birthdays or holidays, can also have reminders set. By default, Outlook may not assign a reminder to all-day events, but you can add one manually:

1. Create a new all-day event or open an existing one.

2. In the event window, check the box labeled "All day."

3. Set the reminder time just as you would for any other event. Note that the reminder time will be relative to midnight of the event date (e.g., a 1-day reminder will notify you at midnight the day before).

Save the event, and your reminder will be set.

Managing Reminders

Effective reminder management involves not only setting reminders but also knowing how to handle them when they appear.

Snoozing Reminders

When a reminder pops up, you have the option to snooze it. Snoozing a reminder delays the notification for a specified period. Here's how you can snooze a reminder:

1. When the reminder alert appears, select the snooze time from the dropdown menu in the reminder window. Options range from 5 minutes to 2 weeks.

2. Click "Snooze." The reminder will reappear after the selected period.

Dismissing Reminders

If you no longer need a reminder, you can dismiss it:

1. When the reminder alert appears, click "Dismiss."

2. The reminder will be removed, and you will not receive any further notifications for that event.

Viewing and Managing All Reminders

You can view and manage all your active reminders from one place:

1. Go to the "View" tab in the Outlook ribbon.

2. Click on "Reminders Window" to open a list of all active reminders.

3. From this window, you can snooze or dismiss reminders as needed.

Best Practices for Using Calendar Reminders

To make the most out of Outlook's reminder features, consider the following best practices:

1. Set Realistic Reminder Times: Choose reminder times that give you enough notice to act on the event. For example, setting a reminder 15 minutes before a meeting might be sufficient, but you might need a day's notice for a significant deadline.

2. Avoid Overloading with Reminders: Too many reminders can lead to notification fatigue. Be selective about which events require reminders to ensure that each alert you receive is meaningful.

3. Use Different Reminder Types for Different Events: Customize reminder settings based on the importance and nature of the event. For instance, use sound alerts for high-priority meetings and pop-up notifications for regular tasks.

4. Regularly Review and Update Your Reminders: Periodically check your reminders to ensure they are still relevant. Remove or adjust reminders for events that have changed or are no longer applicable.

5. Leverage Recurring Reminders for Routine Tasks: For tasks that occur regularly, such as weekly team meetings or monthly reports, set recurring reminders to automate the process.

By effectively setting and managing calendar reminders in Outlook, you can ensure that you stay organized and on top of your schedule, improving both your productivity and time management.

5.4.2 Managing Reminders

Managing reminders in Outlook is crucial for maintaining an organized schedule and ensuring that no important events or deadlines are missed. This section will cover the various aspects of managing reminders effectively, including customizing reminder settings, dismissing and snoozing reminders, and troubleshooting common reminder issues.

Customizing Reminder Settings

Outlook provides several options for customizing reminder settings to fit your personal or professional needs. Here are the steps to access and customize these settings:

1. Accessing Reminder Settings:

  - Open Outlook and click on the "File" tab in the top-left corner.

  - Select "Options" from the list on the left-hand side.

  - In the "Outlook Options" window, click on "Calendar" to view calendar settings.

  - Scroll down to the "Calendar options" section, where you will find various settings related to reminders.

2. Default Reminder Time:

  - The default reminder time determines how far in advance you receive reminders for appointments and meetings.

  - To set this, find the "Default reminders" checkbox in the "Calendar options" section.

  - Check the box and select your preferred time interval from the dropdown menu (e.g., 15 minutes, 30 minutes, 1 hour).

3. Reminder Sound:

- Customize the sound that plays when a reminder appears by clicking on the "Browse" button next to the "Play this sound" option.

- Choose a sound file from your computer that you find suitable and click "OK" to set it.

4. Reminders for All-Day Events:

  - By default, reminders for all-day events are set to 18 hours before the event.

  - You can change this by selecting a different time from the "All day event default reminders" dropdown menu.

Dismissing and Snoozing Reminders

When a reminder pops up, you have the option to either dismiss it or snooze it. Understanding how to use these options effectively can help you stay on top of your schedule without being overwhelmed by constant notifications.

1. Dismissing Reminders:

  - When you dismiss a reminder, it will not appear again for that particular event.

  - To dismiss a reminder, click on the "Dismiss" button in the reminder window.

  - If you want to dismiss all reminders currently shown, click on the "Dismiss All" button.

2. Snoozing Reminders:

  - Snoozing a reminder temporarily hides it, but it will reappear after a specified period.

  - To snooze a reminder, click on the "Snooze" button in the reminder window.

  - A dropdown menu will appear, allowing you to choose how long you want to snooze the reminder (e.g., 5 minutes, 10 minutes, 1 hour).

  - Select the desired snooze interval, and the reminder will reappear after that time.

Managing Multiple Reminders

Outlook allows you to manage multiple reminders at once, which is particularly useful if you have a busy schedule with many appointments and meetings.

1. Viewing All Active Reminders:

- To view all active reminders, click on the "View Reminders Window" icon in the toolbar. This will open a window displaying all pending reminders.

- From this window, you can snooze or dismiss reminders individually or in bulk.

2. Organizing Reminders:

- You can sort reminders by due date, subject, or location by clicking on the corresponding column headers in the reminders window.

- This helps you prioritize which reminders need immediate attention and which can be addressed later.

Syncing Reminders Across Devices

With the increasing use of multiple devices for work and personal activities, syncing reminders across devices ensures you never miss an important event.

1. Using Outlook on Multiple Devices:

- Ensure that you are signed into the same Outlook account on all your devices (desktop, laptop, tablet, smartphone).

- Reminders set on one device will automatically sync and appear on all other devices using the same account.

2. Using Outlook with Other Calendar Services:

- If you use other calendar services (e.g., Google Calendar, Apple Calendar), you can set up calendar syncing to ensure reminders appear across platforms.

- In Outlook, go to the "Account Settings" section and add your other calendar accounts to sync events and reminders.

Troubleshooting Reminder Issues

Sometimes, reminders may not work as expected due to various issues. Here are some common problems and their solutions:

1. Reminders Not Appearing:

- Ensure that reminders are enabled in your Outlook settings.

- Check if the reminder time has passed, and the reminder was automatically dismissed.

- Make sure your device's notification settings allow Outlook to show notifications.

2. Reminder Sound Not Playing:

  - Verify that your device's volume is not muted and that the sound file set for reminders is accessible.

  - Test the reminder sound in the "Calendar options" section of Outlook to ensure it is working correctly.

3. Reminders for All-Day Events Not Working:

  - Check the default reminder time for all-day events and adjust it if necessary.

  - Ensure that the all-day event is set correctly in your calendar.

Using Reminders for Task Management

In addition to calendar events, Outlook reminders can also be used for managing tasks, ensuring you stay on top of your to-do list.

1. Setting Task Reminders:

  - Open the "Tasks" section in Outlook.

  - Create a new task and set a due date.

  - In the task details, enable the reminder option and set the desired reminder time.

2. Managing Task Reminders:

  - Task reminders will appear alongside calendar reminders.

  - You can snooze or dismiss task reminders using the same methods as for calendar events.

Best Practices for Using Reminders

To get the most out of Outlook reminders, consider the following best practices:

1. Set Realistic Reminder Times:

   - Choose reminder times that give you enough notice to prepare for events without overwhelming you with too many notifications.

   - For critical meetings or deadlines, consider setting multiple reminders at different intervals.

2. Keep Your Calendar Updated:

   - Regularly update your calendar with new events and deadlines to ensure all important dates have reminders set.

   - Delete or archive old events to keep your calendar clean and organized.

3. Use Categories and Flags:

   - Categorize and flag important events and tasks to make them stand out in your calendar and task list.

   - This helps you quickly identify high-priority items that need immediate attention.

4. Review Reminders Daily:

   - Make it a habit to review your reminders at the start and end of each day.

   - This ensures you are aware of upcoming events and can plan your day accordingly.

By effectively managing reminders in Outlook, you can ensure that you never miss an important event or deadline, leading to a more organized and productive workflow. Remember to customize reminder settings to fit your personal preferences, snooze or dismiss reminders as needed, and troubleshoot any issues that may arise to keep your reminders working smoothly.

CHAPTER VI
Tasks and To-Do Lists

6.1 Exploring Real-Time Data Use Cases

Outlook's task management features provide a robust platform for organizing your work and personal responsibilities. By using tasks, you can keep track of deadlines, prioritize activities, and ensure that nothing falls through the cracks. This section will guide you through creating, managing, and optimizing your tasks within Outlook.

6.1.1 Adding New Tasks

Creating new tasks in Outlook is a straightforward process that can significantly enhance your productivity. Follow these steps to add new tasks to your Outlook:

Step 1: Accessing the Tasks Module

1. Open Outlook: Start by launching the Outlook application on your computer.

2. Navigate to Tasks: In the bottom navigation pane, you will find an icon labeled "Tasks." Click on this icon to switch to the Tasks view. If you don't see it, you may need to click on the three dots (...) to find the Tasks option.

Step 2: Creating a New Task

1. New Task Button: In the Home tab of the Tasks module, click on the "New Task" button. This will open a new task window where you can input the details of your task.

2. Shortcut: Alternatively, you can use the shortcut `Ctrl + Shift + K` to quickly open a new task window.

Step 3: Entering Task Details

1. Subject: The subject is the title of your task. Enter a brief and descriptive name that summarizes the task. For example, "Prepare Monthly Sales Report."

2. Due Date: Set a due date for your task to ensure you complete it on time. Click on the calendar icon next to the due date field and select the appropriate date. If the task has no specific deadline, you can leave this field blank.

3. Start Date: If applicable, set a start date. This helps you plan when to begin working on the task.

4. Status: The status field allows you to track the progress of your task. You can select from options such as Not Started, In Progress, Completed, Waiting on Someone Else, and Deferred.

5. Priority: Assign a priority level to your task (Low, Normal, High). This helps you prioritize your tasks and focus on the most critical ones first.

6. Reminder: Set a reminder for your task if you want Outlook to notify you at a specific time. Click on the reminder checkbox and choose the date and time for the reminder.

7. Description: Use the large text box to add any additional details or instructions related to the task. This can include steps to complete the task, notes, or any other relevant information.

Step 4: Attaching Files and Links

1. Attachments: If your task requires reference documents or files, you can attach them directly to the task. Click on the "Insert" tab in the task window and select "Attach File." Browse your computer to find the file you want to attach.

2. Links: You can also add links to relevant online resources or documents stored in cloud services. Use the "Insert" tab and select "Link" to add hyperlinks.

Step 5: Categorizing the Task

1. Categories: Assign categories to your task for better organization. Categories in Outlook are color-coded labels that help you group and identify tasks quickly. Click on the "Categorize" button in the task window and choose an appropriate category, or create a new one if needed.

Step 6: Saving and Closing the Task

1. Save & Close: Once you have entered all the necessary information, click on the "Save & Close" button in the task window. Your task is now saved and will appear in your task list.

Step 7: Viewing and Managing Tasks

1. Task List: Your newly created task will appear in your task list. You can view and manage your tasks from this list, sorting and filtering them based on various criteria such as due date, status, and priority.

2. Task Details: To view the details of a task, double-click on it from the task list. This will open the task window, where you can make any necessary updates or changes.

Best Practices for Adding New Tasks

1. Be Specific: When creating a new task, be as specific as possible in the subject and description fields. This ensures you have a clear understanding of what needs to be done.

2. Set Realistic Deadlines: Assign realistic due dates to your tasks. Consider your workload and other commitments to avoid overburdening yourself.

3. Use Reminders: Utilize reminders to keep track of important tasks and deadlines. This helps you stay on top of your responsibilities and avoid missing critical deadlines.

4. Prioritize: Assign priority levels to your tasks to ensure you focus on the most important ones first. High-priority tasks should be addressed promptly, while low-priority tasks can be scheduled accordingly.

5. Organize with Categories: Use categories to group related tasks together. This can be especially useful if you are managing multiple projects or areas of responsibility.

Examples of Task Creation

1. Work-Related Task:

   - Subject: "Submit Project Proposal"

   - Due Date: "July 30, 2024"

   - Start Date: "July 25, 2024"

   - Status: "Not Started"

   - Priority: "High"

   - Reminder: "July 29, 2024, 10:00 AM"

   - Description: "Prepare and submit the project proposal to the client by the end of the month. Include all relevant data and research findings."

2. Personal Task:

   - Subject: "Buy Groceries"

   - Due Date: "July 15, 2024"

   - Start Date: "July 14, 2024"

   - Status: "Not Started"

   - Priority: "Normal"

   - Reminder: "July 15, 2024, 9:00 AM"

   - Description: "Purchase vegetables, fruits, milk, bread, and other essentials for the week."

3. Recurring Task:

   - Subject: "Weekly Team Meeting"

   - Due Date: "July 17, 2024"

   - Start Date: "July 17, 2024"

- Status: "Not Started"

- Priority: "Normal"

- Reminder: "July 17, 2024, 8:30 AM"

- Description: "Attend the weekly team meeting to discuss project updates and next steps. Prepare your status report beforehand."

By following these steps and best practices, you can efficiently create and manage tasks in Outlook, ensuring you stay organized and on top of your responsibilities. The next section will cover how to edit and update tasks, allowing you to keep your task list current and relevant.

6.1.2 Editing and Updating Tasks

Editing and updating tasks in Outlook is a crucial aspect of task management, allowing you to keep your task list accurate and reflective of your current priorities and progress. This process involves modifying various elements of a task such as its title, description, due date, priority, status, and more. In this section, we will delve into the detailed steps and best practices for editing and updating tasks in Outlook.

Accessing Tasks for Editing

1. Open the Tasks Module: To begin editing a task, you need to navigate to the Tasks module in Outlook. You can do this by clicking on the "Tasks" icon in the navigation pane at the bottom of the Outlook window. This will bring up your task list and any task folders you have created.

2. Select the Task to Edit: Browse through your list of tasks and find the one you wish to edit. You can either scroll through your task list or use the search function to locate a specific task. Once you have found the task, click on it to open it in the task window.

Editing Task Details

3. Task Title: The task title is the most visible part of your task and should clearly describe the task at hand. To edit the title, simply click on the task title field and type in the new title. Make sure the title remains concise yet descriptive enough to remind you of the task's purpose.

4. Task Description: The description field allows you to add more detailed information about the task. This is useful for tasks that require multiple steps or additional context. Click on the description field and type in any updates or additional information. Use bullet points or numbered lists if necessary to organize the information clearly.

5. Due Date and Start Date: Adjusting the due date and start date is essential for proper time management. To change these dates, click on the calendar icon next to the due date or start date field and select the new date from the calendar that appears. Setting realistic dates helps you stay on track and prioritize tasks appropriately.

6. Priority: Tasks can be assigned different priority levels (Low, Normal, High) to help you focus on the most important ones. To change the priority of a task, click on the priority dropdown menu and select the appropriate priority level. It is a good practice to regularly review and adjust priorities as your workload changes.

7. Status and Progress: Keeping the status of your tasks updated is crucial for tracking progress. The status options typically include Not Started, In Progress, Completed, Waiting on Someone Else, and Deferred. Click on the status dropdown menu and select the current status of the task. Additionally, you can update the percentage complete by clicking on the progress bar and dragging it to the desired percentage.

8. Categories: Categorizing tasks allows for better organization and filtering. To assign or change a category, click on the "Categorize" button and select the desired category. You can also create new categories if needed by selecting "All Categories" and then "New".

9. Reminders: Setting reminders helps ensure you do not forget important tasks. To add or modify a reminder, click on the "Reminder" checkbox and set the reminder date and time. Outlook will notify you at the specified time, helping you stay on top of your to-do list.

Saving Updates

10. Save Changes: Once you have made all the necessary edits, save your changes by clicking the "Save & Close" button. If you need to make further adjustments or check additional details, you can always reopen the task later.

Best Practices for Updating Tasks

1. Regular Reviews: Make it a habit to review your task list regularly, ideally daily or weekly. This ensures that your task list remains up-to-date and reflective of your current priorities and workload.

2. Clear and Concise Updates: When updating task details, aim to keep the information clear and concise. Avoid adding unnecessary details that could clutter the task description and make it harder to understand.

3. Use Categories and Flags Effectively: Utilize categories and flags to organize tasks and highlight important ones. This makes it easier to sort and filter tasks, especially when managing a large number of tasks.

4. Adjust Deadlines as Needed: If you find that certain tasks cannot be completed by their original due dates, do not hesitate to adjust the deadlines. It is better to set realistic timelines than to miss deadlines consistently.

5. Track Progress Accurately: Update the status and progress percentage of tasks accurately. This helps you and any team members who may be tracking your progress to have a clear understanding of what has been completed and what remains to be done.

6. Set Appropriate Reminders: Use reminders to keep track of critical tasks and deadlines. Ensure that reminders are set at times that give you sufficient notice to act on the tasks.

Example Scenario

Imagine you are managing a project with multiple tasks and deadlines. You have a task titled "Prepare Quarterly Report" with a due date set for the end of the month. As you progress with the task, you realize that some parts of the report require additional data, which will take extra time to gather. Here's how you would update this task:

1. Open the task "Prepare Quarterly Report" in the Tasks module.

2. Update the task description to include details about the additional data needed, specifying the sources and any steps required to obtain the data.

3. Change the due date to give yourself more time, ensuring the new date still aligns with project deadlines.

4. Adjust the priority to High, as this task is critical for the project's success.

5. Update the status to "In Progress" and set the progress bar to reflect the current completion percentage, e.g., 50%.

6. Set a reminder for a week before the new due date to review the progress and make any final adjustments.

7. Save the changes by clicking "Save & Close".

By following these steps, you ensure that your task list remains accurate and that you can manage your tasks effectively, reducing the risk of missing deadlines or overlooking important details.

In conclusion, editing and updating tasks in Outlook is a straightforward process that, when done regularly and effectively, can significantly enhance your productivity and task management capabilities. By keeping your task details current, you ensure that you have a clear and accurate picture of your workload, allowing you to prioritize and complete tasks efficiently.

6.2 Organizing Tasks

6.2.1 Categorizing Tasks

Effectively organizing your tasks in Outlook is essential for maintaining productivity and ensuring that nothing falls through the cracks. One of the most powerful features Outlook offers for task management is the ability to categorize tasks. Categorizing tasks allows you to group similar tasks together, making it easier to prioritize and manage your workload.

Understanding Task Categories

Categories in Outlook are color-coded labels that you can assign to tasks, emails, calendar events, and other items. Each category can represent a different project, priority level, type of task, or any other classification that helps you organize your work. By using categories, you can quickly identify and sort your tasks based on these classifications.

Creating Custom Categories

To get started with categorizing your tasks, you'll first need to create custom categories that align with your organizational needs. Here's how you can create and manage categories in Outlook:

1. Access the Category List:

   - Open Outlook and go to the "Tasks" section.

   - Click on any task to open it.

   - In the task window, look for the "Categorize" option in the toolbar. It is usually represented by a colored square icon.

   - Click on "Categorize" and then select "All Categories" from the dropdown menu.

2. Create a New Category:

- In the "Color Categories" dialog box, you'll see a list of default categories and an option to create new ones.

- Click on the "New" button to create a new category.

- Enter a name for your category that clearly describes its purpose. For example, "High Priority," "Project A," or "Personal Tasks."

- Choose a color for your category from the available options. The color helps visually distinguish different categories.

3. Assign Shortcuts (Optional):

- You can assign keyboard shortcuts to your categories for quicker access. In the "Color Categories" dialog box, select a category and click on the "Shortcut Key" field to assign a shortcut.

4. Save Your Category:

- Once you've named and colored your category, click "OK" to save it.

- Repeat the process to create additional categories as needed.

Assigning Categories to Tasks

After setting up your categories, you can start assigning them to your tasks. Here's how:

1. Open a Task:

- Go to the "Tasks" section in Outlook and open the task you want to categorize.

2. Categorize the Task:

- In the task window, click on the "Categorize" button in the toolbar.

- Select the appropriate category from the dropdown menu. You can assign multiple categories to a single task if it fits into more than one classification.

3. Quick Categorization:

- For even quicker categorization, right-click on a task in the task list and select "Categorize." Then choose the category you want to assign.

Using Categories to Sort and Filter Tasks

Once your tasks are categorized, you can use these categories to sort and filter your tasks, making it easier to manage your workload. Here's how you can utilize categories for better task management:

1. Sort Tasks by Category:

  - In the "Tasks" section, you can sort your tasks by category to group similar tasks together. Click on the "View" tab in the toolbar.

  - Select "Change View" and then "List." This view allows you to see your tasks in a list format.

  - Click on the "Categories" column header to sort tasks by category. Tasks with the same category will be grouped together, making it easier to focus on related tasks.

2. Filter Tasks by Category:

  - Filtering tasks by category helps you focus on specific types of tasks. In the "Tasks" section, click on the "View" tab.

  - Select "View Settings" and then "Filter."

  - In the "Filter" dialog box, go to the "More Choices" tab.

  - Check the "Categories" option and select the categories you want to filter by. Click "OK" to apply the filter.

  - Only tasks with the selected categories will be displayed, allowing you to concentrate on those specific tasks.

3. Using the To-Do Bar:

  - The To-Do Bar in Outlook provides a quick view of your upcoming tasks and calendar events. You can customize the To-Do Bar to show tasks from specific categories.

  - To customize the To-Do Bar, click on the "View" tab and select "To-Do Bar."

  - Choose "Options" and then "Tasks." In the "Tasks" options, you can select which categories of tasks to display in the To-Do Bar.

Best Practices for Categorizing Tasks

To make the most of task categorization in Outlook, consider the following best practices:

1. Consistent Naming Conventions:

  - Use clear and consistent names for your categories. This makes it easier to remember and recognize what each category represents.

2. Limit the Number of Categories:

  - While it's helpful to have categories for different types of tasks, avoid creating too many categories. Too many categories can lead to confusion and make it harder to manage your tasks.

3. Regularly Review and Update Categories:

  - Periodically review your categories to ensure they still align with your organizational needs. Update or consolidate categories as necessary to keep your system efficient.

4. Use Colors Effectively:

  - Choose distinct colors for each category to quickly differentiate them at a glance. Avoid using similar colors for different categories, as this can cause confusion.

5. Combine Categories with Other Tools:

  - Combine categories with other Outlook tools, such as flags, due dates, and reminders, to create a comprehensive task management system. For example, you can use categories to group tasks and flags to indicate their urgency.

6. Leverage Categories Across Outlook:

  - Remember that categories can be used not just for tasks, but also for emails, calendar events, and contacts. Consistently using categories across different Outlook items can help you maintain a cohesive organizational system.

Examples of Effective Task Categories

To provide some inspiration, here are examples of effective task categories that you might consider using:

1. Priority-Based Categories:

   - High Priority

   - Medium Priority

   - Low Priority

2. Project-Based Categories:

   - Project A

   - Project B

   - Project C

3. Time-Based Categories:

   - Daily Tasks

   - Weekly Tasks

   - Monthly Tasks

4. Type-Based Categories:

   - Meetings

   - Follow-Ups

   - Research

5. Personal and Professional Categories:

   - Work

   - Personal

   - Family

By categorizing your tasks effectively, you can significantly enhance your productivity and ensure that you stay on top of your workload. Categories provide a powerful way to organize, prioritize, and manage your tasks, helping you to focus on what's most important and achieve your goals efficiently.

6.2.2 Prioritizing Tasks

Prioritizing tasks is a critical aspect of task management. It involves determining the importance and urgency of each task and arranging them in a way that ensures you focus on the most critical tasks first. Here are some strategies and features in Outlook that can help you prioritize your tasks effectively.

1. Understanding Task Prioritization

Before diving into the tools and features Outlook offers, it's important to understand the basics of task prioritization. Tasks can generally be categorized into four priority levels based on their urgency and importance:

- High Priority: Tasks that are both urgent and important. These tasks need immediate attention and should be at the top of your list.

- Medium Priority: Tasks that are important but not urgent. These tasks should be scheduled appropriately to ensure they are completed on time.

- Low Priority: Tasks that are urgent but not important. These tasks can often be delegated or completed quickly to get them out of the way.

- No Priority: Tasks that are neither urgent nor important. These tasks can be postponed or done during downtime.

2. Setting Priorities in Outlook

Outlook allows you to set priority levels for your tasks, making it easier to manage your workload. Here's how you can set and use priorities in Outlook:

- Assigning Priority Levels:

  1. Open your Outlook Task List.

  2. Select the task you want to prioritize.

  3. Click on the "Priority" dropdown menu in the task's details pane.

  4. Choose between "Low", "Normal", or "High" priority.

By assigning a priority level, you can easily sort and filter your tasks based on their importance.

- Using Task Flags:

  Task flags can also help you prioritize your tasks. Flags can indicate the urgency of a task and help you keep track of deadlines. To flag a task:

  1. Right-click on the task.

  2. Select "Follow Up" and choose a flag option, such as "Today", "Tomorrow", or "This Week".

Flags can provide visual cues to help you quickly identify high-priority tasks.

3. Categorizing Tasks for Better Priority Management

Categories can further enhance your task prioritization by allowing you to group similar tasks together. This can help you manage your time more effectively by focusing on one category at a time. To categorize tasks in Outlook:

- Creating and Assigning Categories:

  1. Open your Task List.

  2. Right-click on a task and select "Categorize".

  3. Choose an existing category or create a new one.

For example, you might have categories such as "Work", "Personal", "Urgent", and "Long-Term". By assigning categories, you can filter your tasks to focus on specific types or priorities.

4. Using Due Dates and Reminders

Setting due dates and reminders can help ensure that you stay on top of your priorities. Outlook allows you to assign due dates to tasks, which can then be sorted and filtered to show the most pressing tasks first. To set a due date:

- Assigning Due Dates:

  1. Select the task.

  2. In the task details pane, enter a due date in the "Due Date" field.

Additionally, you can set reminders to alert you before the task is due:

- Setting Reminders:

  1. Click on the task.

  2. In the task details pane, check the "Reminder" box and set the date and time for the reminder.

Reminders will prompt you to take action, ensuring that high-priority tasks are not overlooked.

5. Utilizing the To-Do Bar and Task Views

Outlook's To-Do Bar and customizable task views can help you keep your priorities in sight:

- To-Do Bar:

  The To-Do Bar provides a quick view of your upcoming tasks and appointments. You can configure it to show tasks by priority, making it easier to focus on high-priority items. To enable the To-Do Bar:

  1. Go to the "View" tab.

2. Select "To-Do Bar" and choose "Tasks".

- Customizing Task Views:

Custom views can help you manage your task list more effectively by displaying tasks according to your preferred criteria. To customize task views:

1. Click on the "View" tab.

2. Select "Change View" and choose "Manage Views".

3. Create a new view or modify an existing one to sort tasks by priority, due date, or category.

6. Integrating Outlook with Other Tools

Integrating Outlook with other productivity tools can enhance your task management capabilities. For instance, combining Outlook with Microsoft To Do allows for seamless synchronization of tasks across devices. You can create tasks in Outlook and manage them on the go with the To Do app, ensuring that you stay on top of your priorities wherever you are.

7. Reviewing and Adjusting Priorities

Regularly reviewing and adjusting your task priorities is crucial for effective time management. Set aside time each week to review your task list, adjust priorities, and ensure that your task management system aligns with your current goals and deadlines. This practice helps you stay organized and focused on what matters most.

8. Tips for Effective Task Prioritization

Here are some additional tips to help you prioritize tasks effectively in Outlook:

- Break Down Large Tasks: Divide large tasks into smaller, manageable sub-tasks. This makes it easier to track progress and prevents you from feeling overwhelmed.

- Focus on One Task at a Time: Avoid multitasking, as it can reduce productivity and increase stress. Concentrate on completing one task before moving on to the next.

- Use the Eisenhower Matrix: This matrix helps you categorize tasks based on their urgency and importance, guiding you to prioritize effectively. Tasks are divided into four quadrants: urgent and important, important but not urgent, urgent but not important, and neither urgent nor important.

- Delegate When Possible: If a task can be handled by someone else, delegate it. This frees up your time to focus on higher-priority tasks.

- Set Clear Deadlines: Assign specific deadlines to your tasks. Clear deadlines help you stay focused and ensure that tasks are completed on time.

- Review and Adjust Daily: Start each day by reviewing your task list and adjusting priorities as needed. This helps you stay aligned with your goals and ensures that your task list reflects your current needs.

Conclusion

Prioritizing tasks in Outlook is an essential skill for managing your workload effectively. By understanding the importance of prioritization, using Outlook's built-in features, and implementing best practices, you can ensure that you stay focused on what's most important and achieve your goals efficiently. Regularly reviewing and adjusting your priorities will help you stay organized, reduce stress, and maintain high productivity levels.

6.3 Using the To-Do List

6.3.1 Adding Items to the To-Do List

The To-Do List in Outlook is a powerful feature designed to help you keep track of your tasks and ensure that nothing falls through the cracks. Adding items to your To-Do List is straightforward, but understanding the various ways to add tasks and the options available can greatly enhance your productivity.

Adding Tasks from the Task Pane

One of the simplest methods to add a new task to your To-Do List is by using the Task Pane. Follow these steps:

1. Open the Task Pane:

   - In Outlook, navigate to the "Tasks" section. You can do this by clicking on the "Tasks" icon in the bottom navigation pane or pressing `Ctrl + 4`.

2. Add a New Task:

   - Click on "New Task" in the Home tab, or press `Ctrl + N`. This will open a new task window where you can enter the details of your task.

3. Enter Task Details:

   - Subject: Enter a brief description of the task in the "Subject" field. This should be a concise summary that allows you to quickly identify the task.

   - Start Date and Due Date: Specify when the task should start and when it is due. Setting these dates helps you manage your time effectively.

   - Priority: Set the priority of the task (Low, Normal, High). This helps you focus on tasks that are more urgent.

   - Status: Choose the current status of the task (Not Started, In Progress, Completed, Waiting on Someone Else, Deferred).

- Details: Use the large text box to add more detailed information about the task, including any necessary steps or notes.

4. Save and Close:

- Once you have entered all the necessary information, click "Save & Close." The task will now appear in your To-Do List.

Adding Tasks from Email Messages

Outlook allows you to create tasks directly from your email messages. This is particularly useful for turning actionable emails into tasks without having to manually re-enter all the information.

1. Drag and Drop:

- Select the email message that you want to convert into a task.

- Drag the email from your inbox and drop it onto the "Tasks" icon in the navigation pane. Outlook will automatically create a new task with the email content.

2. Create a Task from an Email:

- Right-click on the email and select "Move to Folder" > "Tasks." This action will open a new task window with the email subject as the task name and the email content in the task details.

- Modify the task details as needed and then click "Save & Close."

3. Quick Steps

Quick Steps is a feature in Outlook that allows you to automate common tasks. You can create a Quick Step to add tasks to your To-Do List quickly.

Create a Quick Step:

- Go to the Home tab and find the Quick Steps group.

- Click "Create New" to open the Edit Quick Step dialog box.

- Name your Quick Step (e.g., "Create Task from Email").

- Select "Create a Task with Attachment" as the action.

- Click "Finish" to save your Quick Step.

Using Quick Steps:

  - Select the email you want to convert into a task.

  - Click on your newly created Quick Step from the Quick Steps group. This will create a task from the selected email and add it to your To-Do List.

Flagging Emails for Follow-Up

Flagging emails for follow-up is another method to add items to your To-Do List. This approach is beneficial for emails that require action but do not necessarily need to be converted into detailed tasks.

1. Flag an Email:

  - In your inbox, right-click on the flag icon next to the email subject.

  - Choose a flag option (Today, Tomorrow, This Week, Next Week, No Date, Custom). The flagged email will now appear in your To-Do List.

2. Manage Flagged Emails:

  - Flagged emails are automatically added to your To-Do List with the flag date as the due date.

  - You can view and manage these flagged emails from the "Tasks" or "To-Do List" views.

Using Keyboard Shortcuts

For those who prefer using keyboard shortcuts, Outlook offers several shortcuts that can streamline the process of adding tasks to your To-Do List.

1. Create a New Task:

  - Press `Ctrl + Shift + K` to open a new task window quickly.

2. Flag an Email for Follow-Up:

  - Press `Ctrl + Shift + G` to open the flag for follow-up dialog box for the selected email.

Adding Tasks via Mobile Devices

Outlook's mobile app also supports task management, allowing you to add tasks to your To-Do List while on the go.

1. Open Outlook Mobile:

  - Launch the Outlook app on your mobile device.

2. Navigate to Tasks:

  - Tap on the "Tasks" icon in the bottom navigation bar.

3. Add a New Task:

  - Tap on the "+" icon to create a new task.

  - Enter the task details and tap "Save."

Integrating with Microsoft To Do

Outlook integrates seamlessly with Microsoft To Do, a separate app that specializes in task management. This integration allows you to add tasks in Outlook and manage them in Microsoft To Do.

1. Accessing Microsoft To Do:

  - Download and install the Microsoft To Do app on your computer or mobile device.

2. Syncing Tasks:

  - Outlook tasks are automatically synced with Microsoft To Do if you are using the same Microsoft account.

  - You can view, edit, and complete tasks in either application, and changes will sync across both platforms.

Setting Task Reminders

Adding reminders to your tasks ensures that you do not forget important deadlines.

1. Set a Reminder:

  - Open the task you want to add a reminder to.

  - Check the "Reminder" box and set the date and time for the reminder.

  - Click "Save & Close."

2. Managing Reminders:

  - You can view and dismiss reminders from the Reminders window that pops up in Outlook at the specified time.

Categorizing and Prioritizing Tasks

Categorizing and prioritizing tasks helps you manage your workload effectively.

1. Add Categories:

  - Open the task and click on "Categorize" in the ribbon.

  - Choose a category or create a new one.

2. Set Priority:

  - Set the priority of the task (Low, Normal, High) in the task window.

Viewing and Managing the To-Do List

Finally, managing your To-Do List involves regularly reviewing and updating your tasks.

1. Viewing the To-Do List:

  - Go to the "Tasks" section and select "To-Do List" from the navigation pane.

2. Updating Task Status:

  - Mark tasks as complete by checking the checkbox next to the task.

  - Edit tasks by double-clicking on them to open the task window.

3. Deleting Tasks:

  - Right-click on a task and select "Delete" to remove it from your To-Do List.

By mastering these methods for adding items to your To-Do List, you can ensure that you stay organized and on top of your responsibilities. Regularly using the To-Do List in Outlook will help you manage your tasks efficiently and improve your overall productivity.

6.3.2 Managing the To-Do List

Managing the To-Do List in Outlook is a crucial skill that helps you keep track of your tasks, prioritize your work, and ensure nothing falls through the cracks. Outlook's To-Do List integrates seamlessly with the Tasks feature, allowing you to view and manage all your tasks in one place. This section will guide you through various aspects of managing your To-Do List effectively.

Understanding the To-Do List Interface

The To-Do List interface in Outlook is designed to provide a comprehensive view of all your tasks and flagged items. Here's a quick overview of the main components:

- Task List Pane: This pane displays all your tasks and flagged items. You can sort and filter tasks based on different criteria such as due date, categories, and priority.

- Reading Pane: The Reading Pane provides detailed information about the selected task. Here, you can view task details, make updates, and mark tasks as complete.

- Task Ribbon: The Task Ribbon contains various commands and tools to manage your tasks, such as creating new tasks, categorizing tasks, and setting task reminders.

Sorting and Filtering Tasks

To efficiently manage your To-Do List, you can sort and filter tasks based on different criteria. This helps you focus on the most important tasks and view your workload in a structured manner.

- Sorting Tasks: You can sort tasks by different attributes such as due date, start date, priority, and categories. To sort tasks, click on the column header in the Task List Pane. For example, clicking on the "Due Date" column header will sort tasks by their due dates.

- Filtering Tasks: Filtering allows you to display only specific tasks that meet certain criteria. For example, you can filter tasks to show only those that are due today or tasks assigned to a particular category. To filter tasks, use the Filter options available in the Task Ribbon.

Setting Task Priorities

Assigning priorities to your tasks helps you focus on the most critical tasks first. Outlook allows you to set three levels of priority: High, Normal, and Low.

- High Priority: Use this for tasks that are urgent and important. These tasks should be completed as soon as possible.

- Normal Priority: This is the default priority level for tasks. Use this for tasks that need to be done but are not urgent.

- Low Priority: Use this for tasks that are not urgent and can be deferred if necessary.

To set the priority of a task, open the task in the Reading Pane or Task Window, and select the appropriate priority level from the Priority dropdown menu.

Adding Categories to Tasks

Categories allow you to organize tasks into different groups based on their nature or project. You can create custom categories and assign them different colors for easy identification.

- Creating Categories: To create a new category, go to the Task Ribbon, click on "Categorize," and select "All Categories." In the Color Categories dialog box, click "New," enter the category name, select a color, and click "OK."

- Assigning Categories: To assign a category to a task, open the task in the Reading Pane or Task Window, click on "Categorize" in the Task Ribbon, and select the desired category.

Setting Reminders

Reminders help you stay on top of your tasks by notifying you when a task is due or needs attention. You can set reminders for any task in your To-Do List.

- Adding Reminders: To add a reminder, open the task in the Reading Pane or Task Window, and check the "Reminder" box. Set the date and time for the reminder. You can also choose to set a sound notification for the reminder.

- Managing Reminders: You can manage reminders from the Task Ribbon. For example, you can dismiss a reminder, snooze it for a later time, or open the task directly from the reminder notification.

Marking Tasks as Complete

Once you complete a task, it's important to mark it as complete to keep your To-Do List up-to-date.

- Marking Tasks Complete: To mark a task as complete, select the task in the Task List Pane and click "Mark Complete" in the Task Ribbon. Alternatively, you can open the task and click the "Mark Complete" button in the Task Window.

- Viewing Completed Tasks: Completed tasks are moved to the Completed Tasks view. To view all your completed tasks, click on "Completed" in the View options of the Task List Pane.

Managing Task Recurrence

For tasks that occur regularly, such as weekly meetings or monthly reports, you can set them up as recurring tasks. This saves you time from manually creating the same task multiple times.

- Setting Up Recurring Tasks: To set up a recurring task, open the task in the Task Window, click on "Recurrence" in the Task Ribbon, and specify the recurrence pattern (e.g., daily, weekly, monthly). You can also set the start and end dates for the recurrence.

- Managing Recurring Tasks: Once a recurring task is created, each instance of the task will appear in your To-Do List. You can manage each instance individually, mark them complete, or modify the recurrence pattern as needed.

Integrating Tasks with Other Outlook Features

Outlook allows you to integrate your tasks with other features such as email and calendar. This provides a seamless experience and helps you manage your tasks more efficiently.

- Flagging Emails: You can flag emails for follow-up, and they will automatically appear in your To-Do List. To flag an email, right-click on the email in your Inbox and select "Follow Up," then choose a flag option.

- Linking Tasks to Calendar Events: You can link tasks to calendar events for better time management. To do this, open the task in the Task Window, and in the Task Ribbon, select "Link to Appointment" to create a calendar event linked to the task.

Deleting and Archiving Tasks

Over time, your To-Do List may accumulate tasks that are no longer relevant. It's important to regularly clean up your To-Do List by deleting or archiving old tasks.

- Deleting Tasks: To delete a task, select the task in the Task List Pane and press the "Delete" key, or right-click on the task and select "Delete."

- Archiving Tasks: For tasks that you want to keep for future reference but do not need in your active To-Do List, consider archiving them. You can create an Archive folder in your Tasks folder and move old tasks there. To move a task to the Archive folder, select the task, right-click, and choose "Move to Folder," then select your Archive folder.

Best Practices for Managing Your To-Do List

Effective management of your To-Do List involves adopting best practices that help you stay organized and productive.

- Review Your To-Do List Daily: Set aside time each day to review and update your To-Do List. This helps you stay on top of your tasks and adjust your priorities as needed.

- Break Down Large Tasks: Large tasks can be overwhelming. Break them down into smaller, manageable subtasks. This makes it easier to track progress and stay motivated.

- Use Descriptive Task Names: Use clear and descriptive names for your tasks. This makes it easier to understand the task at a glance and reduces the time spent figuring out what needs to be done.

- Set Realistic Deadlines: Be realistic about the time required to complete each task. Avoid setting overly ambitious deadlines that can lead to stress and burnout.

- Prioritize Your Tasks: Regularly review your task priorities and adjust them based on your current workload and deadlines. Focus on high-priority tasks first to ensure important work gets done.

By following these guidelines and making use of the features available in Outlook, you can effectively manage your To-Do List and enhance your productivity. Whether you are tracking personal tasks or managing work-related projects, the To-Do List in Outlook provides a powerful tool to keep you organized and on track.

CHAPTER VII
Notes and Journal

7.1 Using Notes

Notes in Outlook function similarly to sticky notes or memos you might keep on your desk. They provide a convenient way to jot down quick thoughts, reminders, or pieces of information that you might need to refer to later. Using notes can help you stay organized and ensure that you don't forget important tasks or ideas.

7.1.1 Creating Notes

Creating notes in Outlook is a simple and straightforward process, but understanding the full functionality can greatly enhance your productivity. Here's a step-by-step guide to creating notes:

1. Accessing Notes: To begin creating a note, you first need to access the Notes section in Outlook. This can typically be found in the navigation pane on the left-hand side of the Outlook window. If you don't see Notes immediately, you may need to click on the ellipsis (...) and select Notes from the dropdown menu.

2. Creating a New Note: Once you are in the Notes section, you can create a new note by following these steps:

   - Click on 'New Note': Look for the "New Note" button in the toolbar at the top of the window. Clicking this button will open a new note.

   - Using Keyboard Shortcut: Alternatively, you can use the keyboard shortcut "Ctrl+Shift+N" (on Windows) or "Command+Shift+N" (on Mac) to quickly create a new note.

3. Entering Content: After the new note window opens, you can begin typing your content directly into the note. The note window resembles a small, yellow sticky note, providing a familiar and intuitive interface.

   - Title and Body: While Outlook notes do not have distinct fields for titles and body text, you can create a de facto title by typing the most important information or a summary of the note at the top, followed by more detailed information below.

   - Formatting: Outlook notes do not support advanced formatting options like bold or italics, but you can still organize your information by using line breaks and spacing.

4. Saving the Note: Once you have entered the desired content, saving the note is automatic. Simply click outside the note window, and it will be saved to your Notes folder. There is no need to manually save each note, as Outlook takes care of this for you.

5. Managing Note Size and Position: You can resize and reposition notes on your screen to suit your workflow:

   - Resizing: To resize a note, click and drag the edges or corners of the note window.

   - Repositioning: To move a note, click and drag the title bar at the top of the note window to the desired location on your screen.

6. Closing the Note: To close the note window without deleting it, simply click the "X" in the upper-right corner of the note. This will close the note but keep it saved in your Notes folder.

7. Viewing and Editing Existing Notes: To view or edit an existing note, return to the Notes section in Outlook. Here, you will see a list of all your saved notes. Simply double-click on any note to open and edit it.

8. Organizing Notes: While Outlook Notes do not have advanced organizational features, you can still keep your notes in order by:

   - Using Consistent Titles: Create a convention for note titles that makes it easy to identify the content at a glance.

   - Categorizing Notes: Although categories are not a built-in feature of Outlook Notes, you can manually add a category keyword to the beginning of each note's content. For example, start all work-related notes with "Work:" and personal notes with "Personal:".

9. Searching Notes: If you have many notes and need to find a specific one, use the search function:

- Search Bar: Type a keyword or phrase into the search bar at the top of the Notes section. Outlook will filter your notes to display only those that contain the search term.

- Filtering Options: Use additional filtering options to narrow down your search, such as sorting by date or alphabetically by title.

10. Using Notes in Different Outlook Versions: The process of creating and managing notes is similar across different versions of Outlook (e.g., Outlook 2016, Outlook 2019, Outlook 365). However, there may be slight variations in the interface and available features.

11. Tips for Effective Note Taking:

- Be Concise: Keep your notes short and to the point. This makes them easier to review and understand later.

- Prioritize Information: Place the most important information at the top of the note.

- Regular Review: Periodically review your notes to keep track of tasks and ideas, and delete or archive notes that are no longer needed.

12. Integrating Notes with Other Outlook Features: Although notes are a standalone feature in Outlook, you can integrate them with other Outlook functionalities:

- Linking to Emails: Copy and paste the content of a note into an email if you need to share it with others.

- Using Tasks: Convert important notes into tasks to ensure they are tracked and completed.

By following these steps and tips, you can effectively use the Notes feature in Outlook to enhance your productivity and organization. Notes provide a simple yet powerful way to capture and manage information, ensuring that nothing important slips through the cracks.

Conclusion

Notes are an invaluable tool within Outlook, providing a flexible and convenient way to manage quick bits of information. Whether you're jotting down a reminder, an idea, or a task, the Notes feature helps you stay organized and efficient. By understanding how to create, manage, and integrate notes, you can maximize your use of Outlook and streamline your workflow.

7.1.2 Organizing Notes

Organizing your notes effectively is vital to maintain productivity and ensure that you can quickly locate the information you need. Here are several strategies and features in Outlook to help you organize your notes:

Categorizing Notes

One of the most efficient ways to organize notes in Outlook is by using categories. Categories allow you to color-code your notes and group them based on their content or purpose. Here's how you can categorize your notes:

1. Assigning a Category to a Note:

  - Right-click on the note you wish to categorize.

  - Select "Categorize" from the context menu.

  - Choose from the list of available categories. If you need a new category, you can create one by selecting "All Categories," then "New."

2. Creating Custom Categories:

  - Click on "Categorize" in the context menu.

  - Select "All Categories."

  - Click "New," name your category, and choose a color.

  - Click "OK" to save the new category.

By categorizing your notes, you can easily filter and sort them, making it simpler to find related notes quickly.

Sorting Notes

Outlook offers several ways to sort your notes to keep them organized:

1. Sort by Date:

 - This default sorting method arranges your notes by the date they were created or last modified. This is useful for keeping track of your most recent thoughts.

2. Sort by Category:

  - To sort by category, click on the "View" tab in the ribbon.

  - Select "View Settings" and then "Sort."

  - Choose "Categories" from the list to sort your notes by their assigned categories.

3. Sort by Subject:

  - You can also sort your notes alphabetically by their subject lines.

  - Follow the same steps as above, but select "Subject" instead of "Categories."

Using the Notes List View

Switching to the list view in Outlook allows you to see all your notes in a tabular format, providing a clear overview. This view shows key information such as the note's subject, creation date, and category, which makes it easier to manage your notes.

1. Accessing List View:

  - Click on the "View" tab in the ribbon.

  - Select "Change View" and choose "Notes List."

2. Customizing Columns:

 - In list view, you can add or remove columns to show more or less information about each note.

  - Right-click on the column headers and choose "Field Chooser."

 - Drag fields from the chooser to the headers to add them, or drag headers away to remove them.

Grouping Notes

Grouping notes is another effective method to keep related notes together. You can group notes by different criteria, such as category or creation date.

1. Group by Category:

  - Go to the "View" tab in the ribbon.

  - Select "View Settings," then "Group By."

  - Choose "Categories" and click "OK."

2. Group by Date:

  - Similarly, you can group by the creation date by selecting "Created" in the "Group By" settings.

Grouping your notes makes it easier to navigate through large numbers of notes and quickly locate relevant information.

Searching Notes

The search feature in Outlook is a powerful tool to locate specific notes quickly. You can search by keywords, categories, or even by specific content within the notes.

1. Using the Search Bar:

  - Simply type your search term into the search bar at the top of the Notes pane.

  - Outlook will display all notes that match your search criteria.

2. Advanced Search Options:

  - Click on the "Search Tools" tab that appears when you start typing in the search bar.

  - Use options such as "Subject," "Body," "Categories," and "Date Modified" to refine your search.

Archiving Old Notes

Over time, you may accumulate a large number of notes. Archiving old notes that are no longer in active use can help keep your workspace uncluttered.

1. Manual Archiving:

- Select the notes you want to archive.

- Right-click and choose "Move to Folder."

- Select or create a folder designated for archived notes.

2. Auto Archiving:

- Set up auto archiving in Outlook by going to "File" > "Options" > "Advanced."

- Under "AutoArchive," configure the settings to automatically archive notes after a certain period.

Backing Up Notes

It's important to back up your notes to prevent data loss. Outlook allows you to export your notes to a file that you can store securely.

1. Exporting Notes:

- Go to "File" > "Open & Export" > "Import/Export."

- Choose "Export to a file" and select "Outlook Data File (.pst)."

- Select the "Notes" folder and choose a location to save the file.

2. Importing Notes:

- To restore notes from a backup, use the same "Import/Export" wizard, but choose "Import from another program or file."

Integrating Notes with Other Outlook Features

To maximize productivity, you can integrate notes with other Outlook features such as tasks and calendars.

1. Linking Notes to Tasks:

- Drag a note to the "Tasks" pane to create a new task with the note's content.

- This is useful for turning quick thoughts into actionable items.

2. Attaching Notes to Calendar Events:

- You can drag a note to a calendar date to create an event or reminder based on the note.

- This integration helps you keep track of important dates and deadlines.

Using Third-Party Add-Ins

Several third-party add-ins can enhance the functionality of Outlook Notes. These add-ins can provide additional features for note-taking and organization.

1. Evernote:

  - Integrates with Outlook to allow seamless note synchronization.

  - Provides advanced search and organization features.

2. OneNote:

  - Microsoft's own note-taking app that integrates deeply with Outlook.

  - Allows you to link emails and notes, and share notes easily.

By leveraging these organization strategies, you can transform your Outlook Notes from a simple jotting tool into a powerful productivity asset. Whether you are managing a few important reminders or a large collection of detailed notes, these techniques will help you maintain order and efficiency in your digital workspace.

7.2 Using the Journal

7.2.1 Creating Journal Entries

Creating journal entries in Outlook is a straightforward process, but it requires a good understanding of what types of activities you can log and how to efficiently manage these entries. Journal entries can be created manually or automatically, depending on your needs and preferences. Here, we will cover both methods in detail.

Manual Creation of Journal Entries

To create a journal entry manually, follow these steps:

1. Open Outlook: Launch Microsoft Outlook and navigate to the Journal. If you don't see the Journal option in your navigation pane, you may need to enable it.

2. Access the Journal: Click on the "Folder" tab in the ribbon, then click on "New Folder." Name the folder "Journal" and set the "Folder Contains" field to "Journal Items." Click "OK" to create the Journal folder.

3. Create a New Journal Entry: In the Journal folder, click on "New Journal Entry" in the "Home" tab. This will open a new journal entry window.

4. Fill in the Details: In the new journal entry window, you will see several fields that you need to fill out:

  - Subject: Enter a descriptive title for the journal entry.

  - Entry Type: Select the type of activity you are logging (e.g., phone call, meeting, task).

  - Start Time and Duration: Enter the start time and duration of the activity. You can also use the timer feature to track the duration of the activity in real-time.

  - Description: Use the large text box to enter any additional details about the activity. This can include notes, outcomes, or any important information related to the activity.

5. Link to Other Items: You can link the journal entry to other Outlook items, such as contacts, emails, or tasks. Click on "Contacts" in the journal entry window and select the relevant contacts. This helps you to quickly reference related items from your journal entry.

6. Save and Close: Once you have filled in all the necessary details, click "Save & Close" to create the journal entry. The entry will now appear in your Journal folder, organized by date and time.

Automatic Creation of Journal Entries

Outlook also allows you to create journal entries automatically for certain types of activities. This can save you time and ensure that important activities are always logged. Here's how to set up automatic journal entries:

1. Open Outlook Options: Go to "File" > "Options" to open the Outlook Options window.

2. Access Journal Options: In the Outlook Options window, click on "Notes and Journal" in the left pane, and then click on "Journal Options."

3. Configure Journal Options: In the Journal Options window, you will see a list of activities that you can automatically record in the Journal. These activities include:

 - Emails you send and receive

 - Meetings and appointments

 - Tasks

 - Phone calls

 - Office documents you create or open

 Check the boxes next to the activities you want to record automatically. You can also select specific contacts for which you want to record journal entries by clicking on "Automatically record these items" and selecting the relevant contacts.

4. Specify Document Types: If you want to automatically record activities related to Office documents, click on "Also record files from" and select the types of documents you want to include (e.g., Word, Excel, PowerPoint).

5. Save and Close: Once you have configured your preferences, click "OK" to save the settings. Outlook will now automatically create journal entries for the selected activities.

Best Practices for Using the Journal

To make the most out of the Journal feature in Outlook, consider the following best practices:

1. Consistent Logging: Make it a habit to log activities consistently. Whether you are doing it manually or automatically, ensure that all relevant activities are recorded in the Journal.

2. Detailed Descriptions: When creating journal entries, provide detailed descriptions. This will help you recall important information later and provide context for each activity.

3. Linking Items: Always link journal entries to related Outlook items, such as contacts, emails, or tasks. This creates a comprehensive network of information that is easy to navigate.

4. Regular Review: Periodically review your journal entries to ensure they are up-to-date and accurately reflect your activities. This is particularly important for tracking billable hours or project progress.

5. Privacy Considerations: Be mindful of privacy when logging activities. Ensure that sensitive information is protected and only accessible to authorized individuals.

Examples of Journal Entries

Here are a few examples of how you might use journal entries in Outlook:

- Phone Call: You have a phone call with a client to discuss a project update. You create a journal entry titled "Phone Call with Client - Project Update," select "Phone call" as the entry type, and log the start time and duration. In the description, you summarize the key points discussed and any action items.

 - Meeting: You attend a team meeting to plan the next phase of a project. You create a journal entry titled "Team Meeting - Phase 2 Planning," select "Meeting" as the entry type, and log the start time and duration. In the description, you detail the meeting agenda, attendees, and key decisions made.

- Task: You complete a significant task related to a project. You create a journal entry titled "Completed Task - Draft Report," select "Task" as the entry type, and log the start time and duration. In the description, you outline the steps you took to complete the task and any relevant outcomes.

By following these guidelines and utilizing the Journal feature effectively, you can enhance your productivity, maintain accurate records of your activities, and better manage your professional responsibilities.

7.2.2 Viewing and Managing Journal Entries

To get the most out of the Journal feature in Outlook, it's essential to know how to view and manage your journal entries effectively. This section will guide you through the processes of accessing your journal, navigating through your entries, organizing them, and utilizing various tools to ensure that your records are well-maintained and easy to reference.

Accessing the Journal

To access the Journal in Outlook:

1. Open Outlook: Launch the Outlook application.

2. Navigate to the Journal: Click on the "Journal" icon in the Navigation Pane. If the Journal icon is not visible, you may need to customize your Navigation Pane to include it. Right-click on the Navigation Pane, select "Navigation Options," and check the box next to "Journal."

Viewing Journal Entries

Once you have accessed the Journal, you can view your entries in various ways. Outlook provides different views to help you organize and analyze your data effectively.

1. Entry List View: This view displays your journal entries in a list format, showing key details such as the subject, entry type, and date/time. To access the Entry List view, go to the "View" tab and select "Entry List."

2. Timeline View: The Timeline view provides a visual representation of your journal entries over time. It's particularly useful for seeing the chronological order of your activities. To access the Timeline view, go to the "View" tab and select "Timeline."

3. Icon View: In the Icon view, your journal entries are represented by icons, making it easy to quickly identify different types of activities. To access the Icon view, go to the "View" tab and select "Icon."

Navigating Through Journal Entries

Outlook's Journal offers several navigation tools to help you locate and review your entries:

1. Date Navigator: The Date Navigator is a mini-calendar that allows you to jump to a specific date. Click on a date in the Date Navigator to display journal entries for that day.

2. Go To Date: Use the "Go To Date" feature to quickly navigate to a specific date. Click on the "Go To" button in the "Home" tab, then select "Date."

3. Search: The search bar in the Journal allows you to find specific entries based on keywords. Enter a keyword or phrase, and Outlook will display matching entries.

Organizing Journal Entries

Keeping your journal entries organized is crucial for effective record-keeping and easy retrieval of information. Outlook provides several tools and features to help you manage your entries:

1. Categories: Assign categories to your journal entries to group related activities. Right-click on a journal entry, select "Categorize," and choose a category. You can create custom categories to suit your needs.

2. Sort and Filter: Use the sorting and filtering options to arrange your entries in a meaningful order. For example, you can sort entries by date, subject, or type. Use filters to display only the entries that meet specific criteria.

3. Custom Views: Create custom views to display your journal entries in a way that best suits your workflow. Go to the "View" tab, select "Change View," and then "Manage Views." Here, you can create, modify, and save custom views.

Editing Journal Entries

Occasionally, you may need to edit an existing journal entry to update its information or correct errors. To edit a journal entry:

1. Open the Entry: Double-click on the journal entry you wish to edit.

2. Make Changes: Update the necessary fields, such as the subject, entry type, or duration.

3. Save: Click "Save & Close" to save your changes.

Deleting Journal Entries

If you no longer need a journal entry, you can delete it to keep your Journal organized:

1. Select the Entry: Click on the journal entry you wish to delete.

2. Delete: Press the "Delete" key on your keyboard, or right-click the entry and select "Delete."

Archiving Journal Entries

To keep your Journal manageable and prevent it from becoming cluttered, you can archive older entries. Archiving moves entries to a separate file, where they can be accessed if needed but are not displayed in your main Journal view.

1. Manual Archiving: To manually archive journal entries, select the entries you want to archive, right-click, and choose "Move to Folder." Select an archive folder or create a new one.

2. Auto-Archiving: Enable auto-archiving to automate the process. Go to "File" > "Options" > "Advanced," and click on "AutoArchive Settings." Configure the settings to archive journal entries based on your preferences.

Using Journal for Project Management

One of the most powerful uses of the Journal is for project management. By logging all activities related to a project, you can maintain a detailed timeline and ensure that no tasks are overlooked.

1. Creating Project Entries: For each significant activity related to a project, create a journal entry. Include detailed notes and categorize the entry appropriately.

2. Reviewing Project Progress: Use the Timeline view to see the chronological order of your project activities. This helps you track progress and identify any delays or bottlenecks.

3. Reporting: Generate reports from your journal entries to provide updates to stakeholders. Export entries to Excel or use the "Print" feature to create physical copies.

Integrating Journal with Other Outlook Features

The Journal can be integrated with other Outlook features to enhance its functionality:

1. Linking Contacts: Link journal entries to specific contacts to maintain a complete history of interactions. Open a journal entry, click on "Contacts," and select the relevant contact.

2. Email Logging: Automatically log emails to the Journal by enabling the option in the Journal settings. Go to "File" > "Options" > "Notes and Journal," and check the boxes next to the items you want to log.

3. Task Integration: Link journal entries to tasks to keep track of task-related activities. Open a task, click on "Insert," and choose "Journal Entry."

Best Practices for Using the Journal

To maximize the benefits of using the Journal in Outlook, consider the following best practices:

1. Consistent Logging: Regularly log your activities to ensure your Journal is up-to-date. Set aside time at the end of each day to review and enter journal entries.

2. Detailed Entries: Include as much detail as possible in each journal entry. This makes it easier to recall the context and specifics of each activity.

3. Regular Reviews: Periodically review your journal entries to assess your productivity and identify areas for improvement. Use the insights gained to adjust your workflow and enhance efficiency.

Conclusion

The Journal in Outlook is a versatile tool that, when used effectively, can greatly enhance your ability to track and manage various activities. By following the guidelines provided in this section, you can ensure that your journal entries are well-organized, easily accessible, and useful for a wide range of purposes, from project management to personal productivity. Make the Journal a regular part of your Outlook routine to take full advantage of its capabilities.

CHAPTER VIII
Outlook Customization

8.1 Customizing the Ribbon

Outlook's Ribbon interface, introduced in Microsoft Office 2007, is designed to make accessing features and commands easier and more intuitive. However, each user has unique needs and preferences, and Outlook allows you to customize the Ribbon to fit your workflow. This section will guide you through adding and removing commands from the Ribbon, so you can tailor it to your specific requirements.

8.1.1 Adding and Removing Commands

Customizing the Ribbon involves modifying the tabs, groups, and commands that are displayed. You can add new commands to enhance your efficiency or remove those you don't use to declutter the interface. Follow these detailed steps to personalize your Ribbon.

Accessing Ribbon Customization Options

1. Open Outlook: Start by opening Microsoft Outlook on your computer.

2. Go to Options: Click on the `File` tab in the top-left corner of the window to open the backstage view.

3. Open Customization Settings: Select `Options` from the menu. In the Outlook Options dialog box, click `Customize Ribbon` on the left-hand side.

Understanding the Ribbon Customization Interface

The Ribbon customization interface is divided into two panes:

- The left pane lists available commands that can be added to the Ribbon.

- The right pane shows the current Ribbon structure, including tabs, groups, and commands.

Adding Commands to the Ribbon

1. Select a Tab: In the right pane, choose the tab where you want to add a command. You can expand the tab to see its groups by clicking the `+` symbol next to the tab name.

2. Choose a Group: Select the group within the tab where you want to add the command. If necessary, you can create a new group by clicking `New Group` below the list.

3. Find the Command: In the left pane, scroll through the list of commands or use the `Choose commands from` drop-down menu to narrow down the list (e.g., Popular Commands, All Commands, or specific categories like File Tab).

4. Add the Command: Highlight the command you want to add, then click the `Add` button between the two panes. The command will appear in the selected group on the right pane.

5. Rearrange Commands: You can adjust the order of commands within a group by selecting a command and using the `Up` and `Down` arrows on the right side.

Example: Adding the "Print" Command to the Home Tab

To add the `Print` command to the `Home` tab:

1. In the right pane, select the `Home` tab.

2. Choose an existing group or create a new one by clicking `New Group`.

3. In the left pane, select `Print` from the list of commands.

4. Click `Add` to move the `Print` command to the selected group in the `Home` tab.

5. Use the `Up` and `Down` arrows to position the `Print` command where you prefer.

Removing Commands from the Ribbon

1. Select a Tab and Group: In the right pane, choose the tab and group from which you want to remove a command.

2. Select the Command: Highlight the command you wish to remove.

3. Remove the Command: Click the `Remove` button between the two panes to delete the command from the Ribbon.

4. Reorganize as Needed: Adjust the remaining commands using the `Up` and `Down` arrows to ensure a logical flow.

Example: Removing the "Categorize" Command from the Home Tab

To remove the `Categorize` command from the `Home` tab:

1. In the right pane, select the `Home` tab.

2. Expand the tab to find the `Categorize` command.

3. Highlight `Categorize` and click `Remove`.

4. Rearrange any remaining commands if necessary.

Creating and Managing Custom Tabs and Groups

In addition to modifying existing tabs, you can create entirely new tabs and groups to organize your commands. This is useful for grouping related commands that you frequently use.

Creating a Custom Tab

1. New Tab: In the right pane, click `New Tab` at the bottom. A new tab, along with a new group, will appear in the list.

2. Rename the Tab: Highlight the new tab and click `Rename`. Enter a meaningful name and click `OK`.

3. Add Commands: Select the new group under your custom tab, then add commands as described earlier.

Example: Creating a "Quick Access" Tab

To create a `Quick Access` tab for frequently used commands:

1. Click `New Tab` in the right pane.

2. Select `New Tab (Custom)` and click `Rename`. Enter `Quick Access` and click `OK`.

3. Select `New Group (Custom)` under the `Quick Access` tab and rename it if desired.

4. Add frequently used commands such as `New Email`, `Reply`, and `Forward`.

Creating a Custom Group

1. New Group: In the right pane, select the tab where you want to add a new group, then click `New Group`.

2. Rename the Group: Highlight the new group and click `Rename`. Enter a descriptive name and click `OK`.

3. Add Commands: Add commands to the new group as described earlier.

Example: Creating a "Meeting Tools" Group in the Calendar Tab

To add a `Meeting Tools` group to the `Calendar` tab:

1. Select the `Calendar` tab in the right pane.

2. Click `New Group` and rename it `Meeting Tools`.

3. Add commands like `New Meeting`, `Cancel Meeting`, and `Respond to Meeting`.

Saving and Resetting Customizations

Outlook allows you to save your customized Ribbon settings or revert to the default setup if needed.

Saving Customizations

1. Export Customizations: Click the `Import/Export` button at the bottom right of the customization dialog box.

2. Export File: Choose `Export all customizations`. Save the customization file to your preferred location.

Importing Customizations

1. Import Customizations: Click `Import/Export`, then select `Import customization file`.

2. Select File: Browse to the saved customization file and open it. Outlook will update the Ribbon to reflect the imported settings.

Resetting to Default

1. Resetting a Single Tab: To reset a specific tab, highlight the tab in the right pane and click `Reset`, then `Reset only selected Ribbon tab`.

2. Resetting All Tabs: To reset all customizations, click `Reset`, then `Reset all customizations`.

Tips for Effective Ribbon Customization

- Keep it Simple: Avoid overcrowding the Ribbon with too many commands. Focus on those you use frequently.

- Group Similar Commands: Organize commands logically within groups to streamline your workflow.

- Use Descriptive Names: When renaming tabs and groups, use clear, descriptive names to easily identify their purpose.

- Backup Customizations: Regularly export your customization settings, especially if you make frequent changes, to avoid losing them.

Customizing the Ribbon in Outlook enhances your productivity by tailoring the interface to your unique workflow. By adding and removing commands, creating custom tabs and groups, and managing your settings, you can create a more efficient and personalized email management experience.

8.1.2 Creating Custom Tabs

Customizing the Ribbon in Outlook to create custom tabs is a powerful way to enhance your productivity by tailoring the interface to your specific needs. Custom tabs can consolidate commands and features that you frequently use, making them more accessible and improving your workflow. Here, we'll provide a comprehensive guide on how to create and manage custom tabs in Outlook.

Introduction to Custom Tabs

Custom tabs in the Outlook Ribbon allow you to group commands and features that are relevant to your tasks. This customization makes it easier to navigate through Outlook and reduces the time spent searching for commands. By creating a custom tab, you can add only those commands that you use frequently, ensuring that your workspace is optimized for efficiency.

Steps to Create a Custom Tab

1. Open Outlook and Access Ribbon Customization:

   - Start by opening Outlook and clicking on the "File" tab in the upper left corner of the window.

   - In the sidebar that appears, select "Options" to open the Outlook Options dialog box.

   - In the Outlook Options dialog box, select "Customize Ribbon" from the list on the left.

2. Create a New Tab:

   - In the "Customize the Ribbon" section, you will see a list of tabs on the right side.

   - Click the "New Tab" button located at the bottom of the list. This action creates a new tab named "New Tab (Custom)."

- You will also see a new group named "New Group (Custom)" within this tab.

3. Rename the Tab and Group:

  - Select "New Tab (Custom)" and click the "Rename" button.

  - Enter a meaningful name for your custom tab, such as "My Tools" or "Quick Access."

  - Similarly, select "New Group (Custom)" and click the "Rename" button.

  - Provide a descriptive name for the group that indicates the type of commands it will contain, like "Email Tools" or "Calendar Management."

4. Add Commands to Your Custom Group:

  - With your custom group selected, use the list on the left side of the dialog box to find commands you want to add.

  - Commands are categorized by tabs and can also be searched using the search bar.

  - Select a command and click the "Add" button to move it into your custom group.

  - Repeat this process for all the commands you want to include in your custom tab.

Organizing Commands in Custom Tabs

Organizing commands in your custom tabs and groups ensures that your most-used features are readily accessible. Here are some tips for effective organization:

1. Group Similar Commands:

  - Place related commands together within the same group. For example, you might group all email-related commands under a group named "Email Tools."

2. Prioritize Frequently Used Commands:

  - Position the commands you use most often at the top of the group. This arrangement minimizes the amount of scrolling and searching required.

3. Use Descriptive Group Names:

  - Choose group names that clearly describe the functions of the commands within. This clarity helps you quickly locate the tools you need.

4. Consider Command Size and Order:

- Some commands can be displayed as large icons, making them easier to identify. Right-click on a command in your custom tab and choose "Large icons" to change its size.

- Arrange commands in a logical order based on your workflow. For instance, place "New Email" and "Send/Receive" commands at the beginning of an email management group.

Managing and Modifying Custom Tabs

Once you've created a custom tab, you might find that you need to make changes to it over time. Outlook allows you to manage and modify your custom tabs easily:

1. Edit Existing Custom Tabs:

  - To modify a custom tab, return to the "Customize Ribbon" section in Outlook Options.

  - Select your custom tab or group, and use the "Add," "Remove," and "Rename" buttons to make adjustments.

2. Rearrange Tabs and Groups:

  - You can change the order of your custom tab relative to other tabs by selecting it and using the "Up" and "Down" arrows on the right side of the dialog box.

  - Similarly, rearrange groups within your custom tab by selecting a group and using the arrows to move it up or down.

3. Remove Unnecessary Commands:

  - If you find that some commands in your custom tab are no longer needed, you can remove them. Select the command in the right list and click the "Remove" button.

4. Reset Customizations:

  - If you need to revert to the default Ribbon configuration, you can reset all customizations. In the "Customize Ribbon" section, click the "Reset" button and choose "Reset all customizations." This action will remove all custom tabs, groups, and command modifications.

Benefits of Custom Tabs

Creating custom tabs in Outlook offers several significant benefits:

1. Improved Efficiency:

  - Custom tabs streamline your workflow by placing frequently used commands within easy reach. This efficiency reduces the time spent navigating through different tabs and menus.

2. Personalized Interface:

  - Custom tabs allow you to tailor the Outlook interface to your specific needs and preferences. You can create an environment that aligns with your unique workflow.

3. Enhanced Productivity:

  - By grouping related commands together, custom tabs minimize distractions and help you stay focused on your tasks. This organization leads to increased productivity and effectiveness.

4. Simplified Navigation:

  - Custom tabs simplify navigation by consolidating essential commands in one place. This consolidation is especially beneficial for users who perform repetitive tasks.

Practical Examples of Custom Tabs

To illustrate the practical application of custom tabs, consider the following examples:

1. Email Management Tab:

  - Group 1: Email Creation

    - New Email

    - Reply

    - Forward

  - Group 2: Email Organization

    - Move to Folder

    - Categorize

    - Flag

  - Group 3: Email Tools

- Spelling & Grammar

- Check Names

- Insert Signature

2. Calendar Management Tab:

  - Group 1: Appointments

    - New Appointment

    - New Meeting

    - New Recurring Event

  - Group 2: Calendar Views

    - Day View

    - Week View

    - Month View

  - Group 3: Calendar Tools

    - Print Calendar

    - Share Calendar

    - Overlay Mode

3. Task Management Tab:

  - Group 1: Task Creation

    - New Task

    - New Task from Email

  - Group 2: Task Organization

    - Categorize

- Set Due Date

- Mark Complete

- Group 3: Task Tools

- Assign Task

- Send Status Report

- Task Details

By using these examples as a starting point, you can create custom tabs tailored to your specific needs and tasks, enhancing your overall Outlook experience.

Conclusion

Customizing the Ribbon in Outlook by creating custom tabs is a powerful way to enhance your productivity and streamline your workflow. By following the steps outlined in this guide, you can create custom tabs that are tailored to your unique needs and preferences. Organizing commands within these tabs will make it easier to navigate through Outlook, ultimately improving your efficiency and effectiveness. Take the time to experiment with different configurations, and you'll soon find that custom tabs are an invaluable tool in your Outlook arsenal.

8.2 Customizing the Navigation Pane

The Navigation Pane in Outlook is an essential feature that provides easy access to your email folders, calendar, contacts, tasks, and more. Customizing this pane allows you to tailor Outlook to better fit your workflow and personal preferences. In this section, we'll explore how to adjust the size of the Navigation Pane to optimize your workspace.

8.2.1 Adjusting Pane Size

Adjusting the size of the Navigation Pane can greatly enhance your user experience by providing more space for important elements and reducing clutter. Here's a detailed guide on how to adjust the pane size effectively.

Why Adjust the Navigation Pane Size?

Before diving into the steps, it's important to understand why adjusting the Navigation Pane size can be beneficial:

1. Increased Efficiency: A well-sized Navigation Pane can make it easier to access frequently used folders and items, thus improving your overall efficiency.

2. Better Visibility: Adjusting the size ensures that the names of folders and items are fully visible, reducing the likelihood of misclicks.

3. Personal Preference: Customizing the size according to your preference can make your Outlook experience more enjoyable and less stressful.

Steps to Adjust the Navigation Pane Size

Step 1: Open Outlook

First, ensure that Microsoft Outlook is open and you are in the Mail view. You can access the Mail view by clicking on the Mail icon at the bottom of the Navigation Pane.

Step 2: Locate the Divider

In the Navigation Pane, locate the divider bar. This is a vertical bar that separates the Navigation Pane from the Reading Pane or the main Outlook window. The divider bar allows you to resize the Navigation Pane.

Step 3: Click and Drag the Divider

Hover your mouse cursor over the divider bar until it changes to a double-headed arrow. Click and hold the left mouse button, then drag the divider left or right to adjust the size of the Navigation Pane. Dragging it to the left will make the pane smaller, while dragging it to the right will make it larger.

Step 4: Release the Mouse Button

Once you have adjusted the pane to your desired size, release the mouse button. The Navigation Pane will now stay at this size until you change it again.

Fine-Tuning the Navigation Pane Size

For a more precise adjustment, you can use the following tips:

1. Optimize for Screen Size

Consider the size of your screen when adjusting the Navigation Pane. On larger monitors, you may want a wider Navigation Pane to display more information. Conversely, on smaller screens, a narrower pane might be more practical.

2. Balance Between Panes

Ensure a balance between the Navigation Pane and other panes, such as the Reading Pane and the To-Do Bar. An overly wide Navigation Pane can reduce the space available for reading emails, while a too-narrow pane might cut off folder names.

3. Consider Your Workflow

Think about your workflow and which elements you use most frequently. If you often switch between many folders, a wider Navigation Pane might be beneficial. If you mostly stay within a few folders, a narrower pane could suffice.

Additional Customization Options

Compact Navigation

Outlook also offers a Compact Navigation option that reduces the size of the Navigation Pane icons, providing more space. To enable Compact Navigation:

1. Right-click on the Navigation Pane.

2. Select "Navigation Options."

3. Check the box for "Compact Navigation."

4. Click "OK."

This option condenses the icons into a smaller area, allowing more space for folder names and reducing clutter.

Folder Favorites

You can add frequently used folders to the Favorites section at the top of the Navigation Pane for quick access. To add a folder to Favorites, right-click on the folder and select "Show in Favorites." This keeps your most-used folders readily accessible, regardless of the Navigation Pane size.

Minimizing the Navigation Pane

For an even cleaner workspace, you can minimize the Navigation Pane when not in use. Click the arrow in the upper-right corner of the Navigation Pane to minimize it. When minimized, the pane will collapse into a vertical bar with icons, which you can click to expand when needed.

Troubleshooting and Tips

Pane Resizing Issues

If you encounter issues while resizing the Navigation Pane, such as the pane not staying at the desired size, try restarting Outlook. This can often resolve minor glitches.

Restore Default Layout

If you wish to revert to the default Navigation Pane size and layout, follow these steps:

1. Right-click on the Navigation Pane.

2. Select "Navigation Options."

3. Click "Reset."

4. Confirm the action.

This will restore the Navigation Pane to its original settings.

Using Keyboard Shortcuts

For users who prefer keyboard shortcuts, Outlook offers several commands to navigate and manage the Navigation Pane efficiently. For example:

- Ctrl + 1: Switch to Mail view.

- Ctrl + 2: Switch to Calendar view.

- Ctrl + 3: Switch to Contacts view.

- Ctrl + 4: Switch to Tasks view.

These shortcuts can speed up your navigation within Outlook, making it easier to manage your workflow.

Conclusion

Customizing the Navigation Pane, especially adjusting its size, is a simple yet powerful way to enhance your Outlook experience. By tailoring the pane to fit your needs, you can improve your efficiency, ensure better visibility of important folders, and create a more personalized and enjoyable workspace.

In the next section, we will explore adding shortcuts to the Navigation Pane, further customizing your Outlook setup to streamline your daily tasks.

8.2.2 Adding Shortcuts

Shortcuts in the Navigation Pane provide quick access to frequently used folders, saving time and improving efficiency in navigating through Outlook. You can customize these shortcuts to include folders that are important to your workflow, such as specific email folders, calendar views, or task lists.

Steps to Add Shortcuts:

1. Adding a Folder Shortcut:

   - Right-click anywhere in the Navigation Pane and select "Add New Group" or "Add New Shortcut" (depending on your version of Outlook).

   - Choose "New Folder" to create a shortcut to a specific folder, such as your Inbox, Sent Items, or any custom folder you've created.

   - Select the folder you want to add as a shortcut and click OK.

2. Customizing Shortcut Names:

   - Once added, you can customize the name of the shortcut by right-clicking on it and selecting "Rename."

   - Enter a descriptive name that helps you quickly identify the folder.

3. Reordering Shortcuts:

  - To reorder shortcuts, click and drag the shortcut to the desired position within the Navigation Pane.

  - Release the mouse button when the shortcut is in the desired location.

4. Removing Shortcuts:

  - If you no longer need a shortcut, right-click on it and select "Remove Shortcut" or "Delete" to remove it from the Navigation Pane.

Benefits of Customizing the Navigation Pane

Customizing the Navigation Pane in Outlook offers several benefits:

- Improved Efficiency: Access frequently used folders and features with fewer clicks, saving time navigating through Outlook.

- Personalization: Tailor Outlook to your specific workflow and preferences by organizing shortcuts and adjusting the layout.

- Enhanced Organization: Keep important folders and views readily accessible, reducing clutter and improving productivity.

By leveraging these customization options, you can optimize your Outlook experience, making it more intuitive and aligned with your daily tasks and communication needs.

In conclusion, customizing the Navigation Pane in Outlook allows you to streamline your workflow, prioritize tasks efficiently, and navigate through emails, calendars, and other features with ease. Adjusting pane size and adding shortcuts are essential steps towards creating a personalized Outlook environment that maximizes productivity and enhances user experience.

8.3 Using Outlook Themes

Outlook themes offer a way to personalize your email experience, enhancing both aesthetics and functionality. Themes in Outlook allow you to customize the appearance of your email interface, providing a consistent look across different elements like emails, calendar, and tasks. Here's how you can apply and customize themes in Outlook:

8.3.1 Applying Themes

Applying a theme in Outlook is straightforward and can significantly alter the visual presentation of your mailbox. Themes are designed to coordinate colors, fonts, and graphic effects, creating a unified look that suits your preferences or corporate branding.

Steps to Apply a Theme:

1. Open Outlook: Launch Outlook and navigate to the File tab at the top-left corner of the screen.

2. Access Account Information: Click on Account Information in the left pane. You'll find options for managing your account settings and preferences.

3. Select Options: Within the Account Information screen, click on Options. This will open the Outlook Options dialog box.

4. Navigate to the General Settings: In the Outlook Options dialog box, select General in the left sidebar. Here, you will find various settings related to Outlook's general behavior and appearance.

5. Choose Office Theme: Scroll down to the section labeled Personalize your copy of Microsoft Office. Click on the drop-down menu under Office Theme to reveal available options.

6. Select a Theme: Choose a theme from the available options (e.g., Colorful, Dark Gray, Black) by clicking on it. The preview on the right side will update to show how each theme affects the appearance of Outlook.

7. Apply the Theme: Once you've selected the desired theme, click OK at the bottom of the Outlook Options dialog box to apply the changes. Outlook will immediately update to reflect the new theme across all its components.

Benefits of Using Themes:

- Enhanced Visual Appeal: Themes in Outlook provide a visually appealing interface that can make working with emails, calendars, and tasks more enjoyable.

- Consistency Across Devices: Applying a theme ensures a consistent look and feel across different devices and platforms where you access Outlook, maintaining a professional appearance.

- Accessibility Considerations: Some themes are designed with accessibility features in mind, such as high contrast options, making it easier for users with visual impairments to navigate Outlook.

Customizing Themes

Beyond simply applying themes, Outlook allows for further customization to tailor the appearance to your specific needs:

Customizing Theme Elements:

- Font Settings: Adjust font sizes and styles used throughout Outlook to improve readability and personal comfort.

- Graphic Effects: Some themes offer graphic effects such as gradients or shadows. You can enable or disable these effects based on your preference for visual simplicity or enhanced design elements.

- Background Options: Certain themes allow for background customization, such as setting a background image or color for the Outlook window or specific elements like email messages.

Creating Custom Themes:

For advanced users or organizations wanting a unique look:

- Theme Builder Tools: Microsoft offers tools and guidelines for creating custom Office themes using XML files. This allows businesses to apply corporate branding, ensuring a cohesive look across all communications.

- Deploying Custom Themes: IT administrators can deploy custom themes across a network, ensuring consistency and brand compliance throughout the organization.

Conclusion

By leveraging Outlook's theme customization options, users can personalize their email environment to reflect their preferences and enhance productivity. Whether choosing a predefined theme or creating a custom design, Outlook's flexibility ensures that users can optimize their workflow while maintaining a visually appealing interface.

8.3.2 Customizing Themes

Customizing themes in Outlook allows you to personalize your email experience by adjusting the visual appearance to suit your preferences or corporate branding. Themes in Outlook include combinations of colors, fonts, and effects that can be applied uniformly across your emails, calendars, and other elements within the application.

Benefits of Customizing Themes

Customizing themes not only enhances the visual appeal of Outlook but also contributes to improved readability and user experience. Here are several benefits of using customized themes:

1. Brand Consistency: Organizations can maintain brand consistency by applying company-specific colors and fonts to outgoing emails and calendar invites.

2. Personalization: Users can tailor the appearance of Outlook to reflect their personal style, making the interface more engaging and user-friendly.

3. Visual Clarity: Choosing appropriate color schemes and font styles can enhance readability and reduce eye strain, especially during prolonged use.

4. Professionalism: Customized themes can give a professional appearance to your emails and other communications, making a positive impression on recipients.

Customizing Themes in Outlook

To customize themes in Outlook, follow these steps:

1. Applying Themes

Outlook offers a range of predefined themes that you can apply with a few clicks:

- Step 1: Navigate to the File tab in Outlook.

- Step 2: Click on Options to open the Outlook Options dialog box.

- Step 3: In the Outlook Options dialog box, select Mail from the left-hand menu.

- Step 4: Under the Compose messages section, click on Stationery and Fonts.

- Step 5: In the Signatures and Stationery dialog box, go to the Personal Stationery tab.

- Step 6: Here, you can choose themes for new emails and replies/forwards under the Theme dropdown menu.

- Step 7: Click OK to apply the selected theme.

2. Customizing Themes

For a more personalized touch, customize existing themes or create your own:

- Step 1: Follow steps 1-5 above to access the Signatures and Stationery dialog box.

- Step 2: Select the theme you wish to customize under Theme.

- Step 3: Click on Font to change the font style, size, and color used in your emails.

- Step 4: Use the Effects, Color, and Advanced tabs to further customize the theme's appearance.

- Step 5: To save your custom theme, click Save As and give your theme a unique name. This allows you to reuse it in future emails or share it with colleagues.

3. Managing Custom Themes

Once you've customized a theme, managing and updating it is straightforward:

- Step 1: To access your custom themes, go back to the Personal Stationery tab in the Signatures and Stationery dialog box.

- Step 2: Click on Theme and select Browse.

- Step 3: Navigate to the location where your custom theme is saved and select it.

- Step 4: Click OK to apply the custom theme to your emails.

Best Practices for Theme Customization

- Consistency: Maintain consistency in color schemes and fonts across your custom themes to uphold professional standards.

- Accessibility: Ensure that your chosen themes are accessible to all recipients, considering factors such as contrast and font size.

- Testing: Test your custom themes across different devices and email clients to ensure compatibility and readability.

By mastering the art of customizing themes in Outlook, you can significantly enhance both the visual appeal and functionality of your email communications. Whether for personal use or corporate branding, customized themes empower you to create a more engaging and professional email environment.

.

CHAPTER IX
Advanced Email Management

9.1 Using Rules to Automate Email Management

Automating email management with rules in Outlook can significantly enhance productivity and efficiency. By setting up rules, you can instruct Outlook to perform specific actions on incoming or outgoing emails based on defined criteria. This section will guide you through creating rules to automate your email management.

9.1.1 Creating Rules

Creating rules in Outlook is a straightforward process that involves specifying conditions, actions, and exceptions for email handling. Follow these steps to create your own rules:

Step 1: Access the Rules and Alerts Dialog Box

1. Open Outlook: Start by launching the Outlook application on your computer.

2. Navigate to the Home Tab: Click on the "Home" tab located on the ribbon at the top of the Outlook window.

3. Access Rules: In the "Move" group, click on the "Rules" button. A drop-down menu will appear.

4. Manage Rules & Alerts: Select "Manage Rules & Alerts" from the drop-down menu to open the Rules and Alerts dialog box.

Step 2: Create a New Rule

1. New Rule: In the Rules and Alerts dialog box, click on the "New Rule" button. This will open the Rules Wizard.

2. Select a Template: The Rules Wizard offers several templates for common rule types. For a custom rule, choose "Apply rule on messages I receive" under the "Start from a blank rule" section. Click "Next" to proceed.

Step 3: Set Rule Conditions

1. Choose Conditions: The next screen displays a list of conditions. These conditions determine which emails the rule will apply to. Check the boxes next to the conditions that match your criteria. For example, you can select "from people or public group" to apply the rule to emails from specific senders.

2. Edit the Rule Description: After selecting the conditions, click on the underlined values in the "Edit the rule description" box to specify details. For instance, if you chose "from people or public group," click on the underlined text to select the specific people or groups.

3. Multiple Conditions: You can select multiple conditions to refine your rule further. For example, you can create a rule that applies to emails from a specific sender with certain words in the subject line.

Step 4: Specify Actions

1. Choose Actions: After setting the conditions, click "Next" to specify the actions Outlook should take when an email meets the conditions. Actions can include moving the email to a specific folder, marking it as read, flagging it for follow-up, or deleting it.

2. Edit the Rule Description: As with conditions, click on the underlined text in the "Edit the rule description" box to specify details for the actions. For example, if you choose "move it to the specified folder," click on the underlined text to select the folder.

3. Multiple Actions: You can select multiple actions for a single rule. For instance, you can create a rule that moves an email to a folder and marks it as read simultaneously.

Step 5: Set Exceptions

1. Choose Exceptions: Click "Next" to specify any exceptions to the rule. Exceptions allow you to exclude certain emails from the rule's actions. For example, you might want to apply a rule to all emails except those marked as important.

2. Edit the Rule Description: Click on the underlined text to specify details for the exceptions, just as you did for conditions and actions.

Step 6: Name and Finish the Rule

1. Name the Rule: On the final screen of the Rules Wizard, type a descriptive name for your rule in the "Specify a name for this rule" box. This will help you identify the rule later.

2. Review the Rule: Review the rule's conditions, actions, and exceptions to ensure everything is correct.

3. Turn on the Rule: Check the "Turn on this rule" box if you want the rule to be active immediately. You can also choose to run the rule on emails already in your inbox by checking the "Run this rule now on messages already in 'Inbox'" box.

4. Finish: Click "Finish" to create the rule. The rule will now appear in the Rules and Alerts dialog box.

Example Scenarios

To better understand how to create rules, let's explore a few example scenarios:

Scenario 1: Organizing Emails from a Specific Sender

Suppose you want to automatically move emails from your manager to a folder named "Manager." Here's how you can create this rule:

1. Access the Rules and Alerts Dialog Box: Follow the steps to open the Rules and Alerts dialog box and click "New Rule."

2. Select a Template: Choose "Apply rule on messages I receive" and click "Next."

3. Set Conditions: Check "from people or public group" and click on the underlined text to select your manager's email address. Click "Next."

4. Specify Actions: Check "move it to the specified folder" and click on the underlined text to select the "Manager" folder. Click "Next."

5. Set Exceptions: If you don't need exceptions, click "Next" without selecting any options.

6. Name and Finish the Rule: Name the rule "Manager Emails" and ensure the rule is turned on. Click "Finish."

Scenario 2: Flagging Important Emails for Follow-Up

If you receive important emails that require follow-up, you can create a rule to flag these emails automatically:

1. Access the Rules and Alerts Dialog Box: Open the Rules and Alerts dialog box and click "New Rule."

2. Select a Template: Choose "Apply rule on messages I receive" and click "Next."

3. Set Conditions: Check "with specific words in the subject" and click on the underlined text to enter keywords like "Important" or "Urgent." Click "Next."

4. Specify Actions: Check "flag message for follow up at this time" and click on the underlined text to set the flag options. Click "Next."

5. Set Exceptions: If you don't need exceptions, click "Next" without selecting any options.

6. Name and Finish the Rule: Name the rule "Flag Important Emails" and ensure the rule is turned on. Click "Finish."

Scenario 3: Deleting Junk Emails Automatically

To reduce clutter in your inbox, you can create a rule to delete emails from known spam senders:

1. Access the Rules and Alerts Dialog Box: Open the Rules and Alerts dialog box and click "New Rule."

2. Select a Template: Choose "Apply rule on messages I receive" and click "Next."

3. Set Conditions: Check "from people or public group" and click on the underlined text to select the spam senders' email addresses. Click "Next."

4. Specify Actions: Check "delete it" to automatically move these emails to the Deleted Items folder. Click "Next."

5. Set Exceptions: If you don't need exceptions, click "Next" without selecting any options.

6. Name and Finish the Rule: Name the rule "Delete Junk Emails" and ensure the rule is turned on. Click "Finish."

Tips for Effective Rule Creation

1. Be Specific: When creating rules, be as specific as possible with conditions and actions to ensure the rule targets the correct emails.

2. Test Rules: Before fully relying on a new rule, test it on a small set of emails to ensure it works as expected.

3. Keep It Simple: Avoid creating overly complex rules that may be difficult to manage or troubleshoot.

4. Review and Update: Regularly review your rules and update them as needed to accommodate changes in your email patterns or priorities.

5. Use Descriptive Names: Give your rules descriptive names to easily identify their purpose and make future management easier.

Creating rules in Outlook is a powerful way to automate email management, saving time and reducing the risk of missing important messages. By following these steps and tips, you can efficiently organize your inbox and ensure that your email management process is both effective and streamlined.

9.1.2 Managing Rules

Managing rules in Outlook is crucial to maintaining an organized and efficient email workflow. Once you have created several rules, you might need to edit, disable, or delete them based on your evolving needs. This section will guide you through the process of managing these rules effectively.

Accessing the Rules and Alerts Dialog Box

To manage your rules, you need to access the "Rules and Alerts" dialog box. Here's how:

1. Open Outlook.

2. Go to the "File" tab on the Ribbon.

3. Click on "Manage Rules & Alerts." This will open the "Rules and Alerts" dialog box, where you can see a list of all the rules you have created.

Editing Existing Rules

Over time, the criteria or actions of your rules might need to be updated. Editing rules ensures they continue to meet your needs without having to create new ones from scratch.

1. Select the Rule to Edit: In the "Rules and Alerts" dialog box, you will see a list of your rules. Select the rule you want to edit by clicking on it.

2. Edit the Rule: Click on the "Change Rule" button, then select "Edit Rule Settings" from the dropdown menu. This will open the "Rule Wizard," where you can modify the conditions, actions, exceptions, and name of the rule.

3. Modify Conditions: Update the conditions to refine what emails the rule applies to. For example, you can change the sender's address, keywords in the subject, or specific recipients.

4. Modify Actions: Adjust the actions the rule takes, such as moving emails to a different folder, marking them as read, or forwarding them to another email address.

5. Modify Exceptions: Change any exceptions to fine-tune the rule's applicability. This is useful for ensuring that certain emails are not affected by the rule.

6. Save the Changes: Once you have made the necessary changes, click "Finish," then "OK" in the "Rules and Alerts" dialog box to save the updated rule.

Enabling and Disabling Rules

You may want to temporarily stop a rule from running without deleting it. Disabling a rule can be useful if you want to troubleshoot or if a rule is no longer needed but might be useful in the future.

1. Select the Rule: In the "Rules and Alerts" dialog box, locate the rule you wish to disable.

2. Disable the Rule: Uncheck the box next to the rule to disable it. The rule will no longer be active but remains in the list for future use.

3. Enable the Rule: To re-enable a disabled rule, simply check the box next to it. The rule will become active again and will apply to incoming emails based on its conditions.

Deleting Rules

If a rule is no longer needed and you want to remove it entirely, you can delete it. This helps keep your rules list clean and manageable.

1. Select the Rule to Delete: In the "Rules and Alerts" dialog box, click on the rule you want to delete.

2. Delete the Rule: Click the "Delete" button. A confirmation dialog will appear, asking if you are sure you want to delete the rule. Click "Yes" to confirm. The rule will be permanently removed from your list.

Reordering Rules

The order in which rules are listed determines the sequence they are applied to incoming emails. You might need to reorder your rules to ensure they work as intended.

1. Select the Rule to Move: In the "Rules and Alerts" dialog box, click on the rule you want to move.

2. Move the Rule: Use the "Move Up" and "Move Down" buttons to reorder the rule. Rules at the top of the list are applied first. Adjusting the order can help resolve conflicts between rules and ensure they are applied in the desired sequence.

Importing and Exporting Rules

You can back up your rules or transfer them to another computer by exporting them. Similarly, you can import rules that have been saved previously.

1. Exporting Rules:

    1. In the "Rules and Alerts" dialog box, click on "Options."

    2. Select "Export Rules."

    3. Choose a location to save the .rwz file, give it a name, and click "Save."

2. Importing Rules:

    1. In the "Rules and Alerts" dialog box, click on "Options."

    2. Select "Import Rules."

    3. Navigate to the location of the .rwz file you want to import, select it, and click "Open."

Best Practices for Managing Rules

Managing rules effectively involves more than just creating and editing them. Here are some best practices to help you maintain an efficient rule system:

1. Review Rules Regularly: Periodically review your rules to ensure they are still relevant and functioning as intended. This helps avoid clutter and keeps your email management system efficient.

2. Prioritize Rules: Place the most important rules at the top of the list. This ensures they are applied first and helps prevent conflicts.

3. Test New Rules: After creating or editing a rule, test it with a few emails to ensure it works as expected. Adjust as necessary.

4. Use Descriptive Names: Give your rules clear and descriptive names. This makes it easier to identify and manage them later.

5. Backup Rules: Regularly export your rules to create backups. This is especially important if you rely heavily on rules for email management.

Troubleshooting Rule Issues

Sometimes, rules might not work as expected. Here are some common issues and how to resolve them:

1. Rule Not Applying:

   - Check Conditions: Ensure the conditions of the rule match the emails you expect it to apply to. Conditions that are too specific or incorrectly set can prevent the rule from being applied.

   - Rule Order: Ensure the rule is in the correct order in the list. If another rule is being applied first and altering the email in a way that affects the subsequent rules, adjust the order.

   - Rule Conflicts: Check for conflicts with other rules. If two rules apply to the same email and perform contradictory actions, only one may take effect.

2. Rule Applies Incorrectly:

   - Refine Conditions: If the rule is applying to emails it shouldn't, refine the conditions to be more specific.

   - Check Exceptions: Ensure the exceptions are correctly set to exclude emails that shouldn't be affected by the rule.

3. Rule Running on Sent Items:

   - Specify Folder: Ensure the rule is set to apply only to incoming items and not sent items. Adjust the conditions or actions as necessary.

Conclusion

Managing rules in Outlook is a powerful way to automate and streamline your email management. By regularly reviewing, updating, and optimizing your rules, you can maintain an organized and efficient inbox that meets your needs. With the ability to edit, disable, delete, reorder, import, and export rules, you have full control over how your emails are handled, ensuring that you stay productive and focused on what matters most.

9.2 Using Search and Filters

9.2.1 Searching Emails

Searching for emails in Outlook is an essential skill that can save you significant time and effort. Whether you need to find a specific message, locate all emails from a particular sender, or retrieve an old attachment, Outlook's search feature is designed to help you accomplish these tasks with ease.

1. Understanding the Search Bar:

At the top of your Outlook interface, you'll find the Search Bar. This is your gateway to finding emails efficiently. The Search Bar is prominently located and easily accessible, making it convenient for users to initiate a search at any time.

2. Basic Search:

To perform a basic search, click on the Search Bar and type in a keyword or phrase related to the email you are looking for. As you type, Outlook will start displaying suggestions and search results that match your query. The search results are categorized by relevance, with the most relevant emails appearing at the top.

For example, if you are looking for an email from a colleague named "John Doe," you can simply type "John Doe" into the Search Bar. Outlook will display all emails containing "John Doe" in the sender's name, subject, or email body.

3. Advanced Search Options:

Outlook's advanced search options allow you to refine your search criteria and narrow down results more precisely. To access advanced search options, click on the drop-down arrow next to the Search Bar. This will open a menu with various search filters and criteria.

3.1. Search by Sender:

If you want to find all emails from a specific sender, you can use the "From" filter. Click on the "From" field and type the email address or name of the sender. Outlook will display all emails sent by that person.

For instance, if you need to find all emails from your manager, you can enter their email address in the "From" field. Outlook will then show all emails sent by your manager.

3.2. Search by Subject:

The "Subject" filter allows you to search for emails based on the subject line. Click on the "Subject" field and enter the keywords or phrases related to the subject of the email you are looking for. Outlook will display emails with matching subject lines.

For example, if you are looking for emails related to a project named "Project Alpha," you can enter "Project Alpha" in the "Subject" field. Outlook will show all emails with "Project Alpha" in the subject line.

3.3. Search by Date Range:

The "Received" filter enables you to search for emails within a specific date range. Click on the "Received" field and select the desired date range. You can choose from predefined options like "Today," "Yesterday," "Last Week," or specify custom dates.

For instance, if you need to find emails received in the last month, select "Last Month" from the "Received" filter. Outlook will display all emails received during that period.

3.4. Search by Attachments:

If you are searching for emails with attachments, you can use the "Has Attachments" filter. Check the box next to "Has Attachments," and Outlook will show only emails that contain attachments.

For example, if you need to find emails with important documents attached, enable the "Has Attachments" filter. Outlook will display all emails with attachments, making it easier for you to locate the necessary documents.

3.5. Combining Search Filters:

Outlook allows you to combine multiple search filters to refine your search further. You can use a combination of sender, subject, date range, and attachment filters to narrow down your search results.

For instance, if you need to find emails from your manager about "Project Alpha" received last month, you can use the following combination of filters:

- "From": Your manager's email address

- "Subject": "Project Alpha"

- "Received": "Last Month"

- "Has Attachments": Checked (if you are looking for emails with attachments)

Outlook will display only the emails that match all these criteria, helping you quickly find the specific emails you need.

4. Search Folders:

Search Folders are a powerful feature in Outlook that allow you to create virtual folders containing emails that match specific criteria. These folders automatically update as new emails arrive, ensuring you always have access to the most relevant emails.

4.1. Creating a Search Folder:

To create a Search Folder, right-click on the "Search Folders" option in the Navigation Pane and select "New Search Folder." A dialog box will appear with various predefined search criteria.

Select the desired criteria from the list, such as "Mail with attachments" or "Mail from specific people," and click "OK." Outlook will create a new Search Folder that automatically includes all emails matching the selected criteria.

4.2. Customizing a Search Folder:

You can also create custom Search Folders based on your specific needs. In the "New Search Folder" dialog box, scroll down to the bottom and select "Create a custom Search Folder." Click "Choose" and then "Criteria" to define your custom search criteria.

For example, you can create a custom Search Folder that includes all emails from your manager with the subject "Project Alpha" received last month. This custom Search Folder will automatically update with any new emails that match these criteria.

5. Search History and Recent Searches:

Outlook keeps track of your search history, allowing you to quickly access previous searches. When you click on the Search Bar, a list of your recent searches will appear below it. You can click on any of these recent searches to repeat the search without having to re-enter the search criteria.

6. Search Contextual Menu:

Outlook's search contextual menu provides additional options to refine your search further. After performing a search, right-click on any email in the search results to access the contextual menu. This menu includes options like "Search Folder," "Categorize," and "Follow Up," allowing you to take specific actions based on your search results.

7. Saving Search Results:

If you frequently search for the same criteria, you can save your search results for quick access in the future. After performing a search, click on "Save Search" in the search contextual menu. Enter a name for your saved search and click "OK." Your saved search will appear in the "Search Folders" section, allowing you to access it with a single click.

8. Troubleshooting Search Issues:

If you encounter any issues with the search functionality in Outlook, there are a few troubleshooting steps you can take to resolve them:

- Ensure that your Outlook is up to date with the latest updates and patches.

- Rebuild the search index by going to File > Options > Search > Indexing Options > Advanced > Rebuild.

- Check your search settings and ensure that all necessary mail folders are included in the search scope.

Conclusion:

Mastering the search functionality in Outlook is essential for efficient email management. By understanding how to perform basic and advanced searches, create Search Folders, and utilize search filters, you can quickly locate specific emails and stay organized. Remember to save your frequent searches for easy access and troubleshoot any issues promptly to ensure a smooth email experience.

9.2.2 Applying Filters

Using filters in Outlook is a powerful way to manage and organize your emails efficiently. Filters allow you to view only the emails that meet certain criteria, making it easier to find specific messages and manage your inbox effectively. This section will guide you through the process of applying filters in Outlook, from understanding the types of filters available to step-by-step instructions on how to use them.

Understanding Filters

Filters in Outlook can be applied based on a variety of criteria, including:

- Sender: Emails from specific people or domains.

- Recipient: Emails sent to a particular person or group.

- Subject: Emails containing certain keywords in the subject line.

- Date: Emails received or sent within a specific date range.

- Attachments: Emails with or without attachments.

- Importance: Emails marked as high or low importance.

- Read/Unread: Emails that have been read or are still unread.

- Categories: Emails that have been categorized with specific labels.

- Flagged: Emails that have been flagged for follow-up.

Applying Filters in Outlook

Applying filters in Outlook can be done using the built-in features of the software. Here's a step-by-step guide to help you get started:

Step 1: Accessing the Filter Options

1. Open Outlook: Launch the Outlook application on your computer.

2. Navigate to Your Inbox: Click on your Inbox or the folder where you want to apply the filter.

3. Click on the Search Box: At the top of your Inbox, you will find the Search box. Click inside this box to activate the search tools.

Step 2: Using the Filter Email Option

1. Filter Email Button: In the ribbon at the top of the screen, you will see a "Filter Email" button. Click on this button to view the available filter options.

2. Choose a Filter Criterion: Select the criterion you want to filter by from the drop-down menu. Common options include Unread, Has Attachments, Categorized, Flagged, and others.

Step 3: Applying Specific Filters

1. Unread Emails: To filter for unread emails, simply click on the "Unread" option from the Filter Email menu. Outlook will now display only the emails that you have not yet read.

2. Emails with Attachments: To find emails with attachments, select the "Has Attachments" option. This will show only the emails that contain attachments, helping you quickly locate files sent to you.

3. Categorized Emails: If you use categories to organize your emails, you can filter by category. Select "Categorized" and choose the specific category you want to view. This will display all emails that have been tagged with that category.

4. Flagged Emails: To view emails that you have flagged for follow-up, select the "Flagged" option. This filter is useful for keeping track of emails that require action.

Step 4: Using the Search Tab

1. Advanced Search Options: Click on the Search tab in the ribbon to access more advanced search options. Here, you can combine multiple criteria to create complex filters.

2. Search Tools: Use the Search Tools to specify additional parameters. For example, you can filter emails by a specific date range, sender, or keyword in the subject line.

3. Search Fields: Enter the desired criteria in the search fields. You can use the "From" field to filter by sender, the "To" field to filter by recipient, and the "Subject" field to filter by subject keywords.

4. Apply the Filter: After entering your criteria, press Enter or click the search icon. Outlook will display the emails that match your specified criteria.

Step 5: Saving Search Queries

1. Save Your Search: If you frequently use the same filters, you can save your search queries for quick access. Click on the "Save Search" button in the Search tab.

2. Name Your Search: Give your saved search a meaningful name so you can easily identify it later.

3. Access Saved Searches: To use a saved search, go to the Search tab, click on the "Saved Searches" button, and select the saved search you want to apply.

Step 6: Creating Custom Filters with Rules

1. Go to Rules: In addition to the built-in filter options, you can create custom filters using rules. Go to the Home tab in the ribbon, click on the "Rules" button, and select "Manage Rules & Alerts."

2. New Rule: Click on "New Rule" to start creating a custom filter.

3. Start from a Template or Blank Rule: Choose whether to start from a rule template or create a blank rule. For more control, select "Apply rule on messages I receive" or "Apply rule on messages I send."

4. Specify Conditions: Define the conditions for your rule. For example, you can create a rule that applies to emails from a specific sender, with certain keywords, or received within a particular date range.

5. Set Actions: Specify the actions to take when the conditions are met. Actions can include moving the email to a folder, marking it as read, flagging it, or deleting it.

6. Finish and Save: Review your rule, click "Finish," and then "Apply" to save and activate it.

Tips for Effective Use of Filters

- Combine Filters: Use multiple filters together to narrow down your search results. For example, you can filter for unread emails with attachments from a specific sender.

- Use Keywords: Incorporate keywords in your filters to find emails related to specific topics quickly.

- Regular Review: Periodically review and update your filters to ensure they remain relevant to your email management needs.

- Organize with Folders: Combine filters with folders to keep your inbox organized. For instance, you can set a rule to move all emails from a particular project into a dedicated folder.

- Leverage Categories: Use categories to label emails and then filter by those categories to streamline your workflow.

Common Scenarios for Applying Filters

1. Project Management: Filter emails related to a specific project by using keywords in the subject line and sender's email address.

2. Client Communication: Use filters to view all emails from a particular client, ensuring you never miss important communications.

3. Meeting Requests: Filter meeting requests and appointments by subject or sender to keep track of all scheduled events.

4. Sales and Marketing: Apply filters to manage promotional emails or inquiries from potential customers.

By mastering the use of filters in Outlook, you can significantly enhance your email management capabilities. Filters allow you to quickly locate important messages, reduce inbox clutter, and stay organized. Experiment with different filter combinations to find the most effective way to manage your emails and improve your productivity.

9.3 Archiving Emails

9.3.1 Manual Archiving

Manual archiving in Outlook allows you to move specific emails or folders to an archive location. This can be beneficial for organizing older emails that you no longer need immediate access to but still want to keep for future reference. Here's a step-by-step guide on how to manually archive emails in Outlook:

Step-by-Step Guide to Manual Archiving

1. Accessing the Archive Feature

  - Open Outlook and navigate to the folder containing the emails you want to archive.

  - Ensure you are in the Mail view by selecting the Mail icon at the bottom of the navigation pane.

2. Selecting Emails to Archive

  - You can choose to archive individual emails, multiple emails, or entire folders.

  - To select multiple emails, hold down the `Ctrl` key (Windows) or `Command` key (Mac) and click on the emails you wish to archive.

  - Alternatively, you can click the first email, hold down the `Shift` key, and click the last email to select a range of emails.

3. Initiating the Archive Process

  - Once you have selected the emails or folders you want to archive, right-click on the selection.

  - From the context menu, choose `Move to Folder` and then select `Archive`. If the `Archive` option is not visible, you may need to create an Archive folder manually.

4. Creating an Archive Folder (If Needed)

- If an Archive folder does not exist, you can create one by right-clicking on your account name in the navigation pane and selecting `New Folder`.

- Name the folder `Archive` and click `OK`.

- Now, repeat the process of moving emails to the newly created Archive folder.

5. Confirming the Archive Location

- After moving the emails, you can verify that they have been archived by navigating to the Archive folder in the navigation pane.

- Ensure all selected emails are present in the Archive folder.

6. Managing Archived Emails

- Within the Archive folder, you can further organize emails by creating subfolders. For instance, you might create subfolders for different years or categories.

- Right-click on the Archive folder, select `New Folder`, and name the subfolder accordingly.

Best Practices for Manual Archiving

1. Regular Archiving

- Set a regular schedule for archiving emails, such as at the end of each month or quarter. This helps keep your inbox manageable and ensures important emails are preserved.

2. Categorize Before Archiving

- Before archiving, categorize your emails to make future retrieval easier. Use Outlook's categories feature to label emails by project, client, or topic.

3. Delete Unnecessary Emails

- Archive only those emails you might need in the future. Delete spam, promotional emails, and other non-essential messages to save space and reduce clutter.

4. Backup Your Archive

- Regularly back up your archived emails to an external hard drive or cloud storage. This ensures that you have a copy of your important emails in case of data loss.

5. Use Descriptive Folder Names

- When creating subfolders within your Archive, use descriptive names that make it easy to locate emails later. For example, instead of naming a folder `2023`, name it `2023 - Project XYZ`.

Troubleshooting Manual Archiving

1. Emails Not Moving to Archive

- If emails are not moving to the Archive folder, ensure you have sufficient storage space in your Outlook account. Check for any error messages that might indicate a problem.

- Verify that you have the necessary permissions to move emails. Sometimes, network or server settings might restrict such actions.

2. Archived Emails Not Visible

- If you cannot see archived emails, ensure you are viewing the correct Archive folder. Check the folder properties to confirm it is not hidden.

- If you are using an Outlook account connected to a server (such as Exchange or Office 365), check your online archive if applicable.

3. Duplicates in Archive Folder

- If you notice duplicate emails in your Archive folder, this might be due to accidental multiple archiving. Review your archiving process and adjust to avoid duplicates.

Conclusion

Manual archiving in Outlook is a powerful tool for managing your email storage and keeping your inbox organized. By following the steps outlined above, you can efficiently archive emails and maintain a clutter-free mailbox. Regular archiving, combined with best practices, ensures that your important emails are always accessible and your Outlook experience remains smooth and efficient.

Understanding the manual archiving process and incorporating it into your routine will help you leverage Outlook's full potential, making email management a less daunting task. As you become more comfortable with archiving, consider exploring other advanced features in Outlook to further enhance your productivity and email organization.

9.3.2 Auto Archiving

Auto Archiving is a feature in Outlook that automatically moves old emails and other items to an archive folder at regular intervals. This helps in managing mailbox size, keeping the inbox uncluttered, and improving Outlook's performance. Here's a step-by-step guide to setting up and managing Auto Archiving in Outlook.

1. Understanding Auto Archiving

Auto Archiving involves two processes: moving old items to an archive location and permanently deleting items whose retention period has expired. The items are moved to an archive file, usually a separate .pst (Personal Storage Table) file. This file can be stored on your local machine or on a network drive.

2. Setting Up Auto Archiving

To set up Auto Archiving in Outlook, follow these steps:

Step 1: Open Outlook Options

- Launch Outlook and click on the "File" tab.

- From the left-hand menu, select "Options."

Step 2: Access Auto Archiving Settings

- In the Outlook Options dialog box, click on the "Advanced" category.

- Scroll down to the "AutoArchive" section and click on the "AutoArchive Settings" button.

Step 3: Configure Auto Archiving Settings

- A new dialog box titled "AutoArchive" will open. Here you can configure the various settings for Auto Archiving.

- Run AutoArchive every [X] days: Check this box to enable Auto Archiving and specify the frequency (e.g., every 14 days).

- Prompt before AutoArchive runs: Check this box if you want Outlook to notify you before it runs Auto Archiving.

- Delete expired items (e-mail folders only): Check this option to permanently delete expired items from your email folders.

- Archive or delete old items: Ensure this option is checked to move old items to your archive file.

- Show archive folder in folder list: This option displays the archive folder in your folder list for easy access.

Step 4: Specify the Default Archive Settings

- Clean out items older than: Choose the age of items to be archived (e.g., 6 months, 12 months).

- Move old items to: Specify the location of your archive file. You can use the default location or browse to select a different location.

- Permanently delete old items: Instead of archiving, this option will permanently delete old items.

Step 5: Apply Settings and Run Auto Archiving

- Click "OK" to save your Auto Archiving settings.

- Auto Archiving will now run at the specified intervals based on your configuration.

 3. Customizing Auto Archiving for Specific Folders

Outlook allows you to customize Auto Archiving settings for individual folders. This is useful if you want different archiving rules for different folders. Here's how to do it:

Step 1: Right-Click on the Folder

- In the folder pane, right-click on the folder you want to customize and select "Properties."

Step 2: Access Auto Archiving Settings for the Folder

- In the folder properties dialog box, go to the "AutoArchive" tab.

Step 3: Configure Folder-Specific Settings

- Do not archive items in this folder: Select this option if you do not want this folder to be archived.

- Archive items in this folder using the default settings: This option uses the default settings configured earlier.

- Archive this folder using these settings: Choose this option to specify different archiving settings for this folder.

  - Clean out items older than: Set the age of items to be archived.

  - Move old items to: Specify a different archive file for this folder if needed.

  - Permanently delete old items: Choose this option to permanently delete old items in this folder instead of archiving them.

Step 4: Save Settings

- Click "OK" to save the folder-specific Auto Archiving settings.

4. Managing Archived Items

Archived items are moved to a separate .pst file, which can be accessed anytime. Here's how to manage and access your archived items:

Accessing Archived Items

- In the folder pane, you will see an "Archives" folder or similar name, depending on your settings.

- Expand the "Archives" folder to view the subfolders and items that have been archived.

Opening an Archive File

- If the archive file is not visible in the folder pane, you can open it manually.

  - Click on the "File" tab and select "Open & Export."

  - Choose "Open Outlook Data File" and browse to the location of your archive .pst file.

  - Select the file and click "OK" to open it.

Restoring Archived Items

- You can move archived items back to their original location or another folder if needed.

  - Simply drag and drop the items from the archive folder to the desired location.

  - Alternatively, right-click on the item, select "Move," and choose the destination folder.

5. Tips for Effective Auto Archiving

Regularly Review Archive Settings

- Periodically review your Auto Archiving settings to ensure they still meet your needs.

- Adjust the archiving frequency and item age based on your email volume and usage patterns.

Maintain Archive File Health

- Archive files can grow large over time. Regularly check the size of your .pst file and consider splitting it into smaller files if needed.

- Use the "Compact Now" feature to reduce the size of the archive file.

  - Go to "File" > "Account Settings" > "Account Settings."

  - Select the "Data Files" tab, choose the archive .pst file, and click on "Settings."

  - In the "Outlook Data File" dialog box, click on "Compact Now."

Backup Archive Files

- Regularly back up your archive files to prevent data loss. Store backups on external drives or cloud storage for added security.

Avoid Over-Archiving

- While archiving helps manage mailbox size, avoid over-archiving. Keep frequently accessed items in your primary mailbox for easy access.

6. Troubleshooting Auto Archiving

Auto Archiving Not Running

- Ensure Auto Archiving is enabled in the Outlook Options.

- Verify that the Auto Archiving frequency is set correctly.

Items Not Archiving as Expected

- Check the age of the items. Ensure they meet the criteria for archiving.

- Confirm that the folder-specific settings do not override the default settings.

Archive File Issues

- If you encounter issues opening the archive file, ensure it is not corrupted. Use the Inbox Repair Tool (Scanpst.exe) to fix any issues.

- Go to the Microsoft Office installation folder, find Scanpst.exe, and run it.

- Follow the prompts to repair your .pst file.

By understanding and effectively utilizing Auto Archiving, you can keep your Outlook mailbox organized and improve overall performance. Regularly review and adjust your settings to ensure they align with your email management needs.

CHAPTER X
Security and Privacy

10.1 Managing Junk Email

Managing junk email is a critical aspect of maintaining a clean and efficient inbox. Junk emails, also known as spam, can clutter your mailbox and make it difficult to find important messages. In Outlook, there are several tools and techniques available to help you manage and minimize the impact of junk email. One of the most effective methods is blocking senders. This section will delve into the details of blocking senders, providing step-by-step instructions and tips to help you keep your inbox free of unwanted emails.

10.1.1 Blocking Senders

Blocking senders in Outlook is a straightforward process that can significantly reduce the amount of spam you receive. When you block a sender, any future emails from that address will be automatically moved to the Junk Email folder. This helps to ensure that your inbox remains organized and free from unnecessary clutter.

Step-by-Step Guide to Blocking Senders

1. Open Outlook: Begin by launching the Outlook application on your computer or mobile device. Ensure you are signed in to your account.

2. Select an Email from the Sender: Navigate to your inbox and find an email from the sender you wish to block. Click on the email to open it.

3. Access Junk Email Options: With the email open, look for the "Junk" option in the toolbar at the top of the screen. In some versions of Outlook, this may be represented by a small icon resembling a stop sign or trash can.

4. Block the Sender: Click on the "Junk" option, and a drop-down menu will appear. Select "Block Sender" from the menu. A confirmation message will appear, indicating that the sender has been added to your blocked senders list.

5. Verify the Block: To ensure that the sender is blocked, you can check the blocked senders list. Go to the "Home" tab, click on "Junk," and then select "Junk E-mail Options." In the Junk E-mail Options dialog box, navigate to the "Blocked Senders" tab. Here, you will see a list of all blocked senders, including the one you just added.

Tips for Managing Blocked Senders

Blocking senders is an effective way to manage junk email, but it is also important to periodically review and update your blocked senders list. Here are some tips to help you manage this process efficiently:

1. Regular Review: Make it a habit to review your blocked senders list regularly. This ensures that legitimate emails are not mistakenly blocked and that your list remains up-to-date.

2. Unblocking Senders: If you discover that you have mistakenly blocked a legitimate sender, you can easily unblock them. Go to the "Blocked Senders" tab in the Junk E-mail Options dialog box, select the sender you want to unblock, and click "Remove."

3. Adding to Safe Senders List: To prevent important emails from being marked as junk, add trusted contacts to your Safe Senders list. This ensures that emails from these contacts always reach your inbox.

4. Using Filters: In addition to blocking senders, you can use filters to automatically sort and manage your emails. Create rules to move certain types of emails to specific folders, reducing the clutter in your inbox.

5. Reporting Spam: If you continue to receive spam from blocked senders, consider reporting these emails to your email provider. This helps improve the overall spam filtering system and reduces the chances of similar emails reaching your inbox.

Understanding the Impact of Blocking Senders

Blocking senders is a proactive approach to managing junk email, but it is important to understand its limitations and impact. Here are some key points to consider:

1. Effectiveness: Blocking senders is highly effective for managing persistent spam from specific email addresses. However, spammers often use multiple addresses, so you may need to block several addresses over time.

2. False Positives: Occasionally, legitimate emails may be mistakenly identified as junk and blocked. Regularly reviewing your blocked senders list helps mitigate this risk.

3. Junk Email Folder: Emails from blocked senders are moved to the Junk Email folder, where they are stored for a limited time before being automatically deleted. Check your Junk Email folder periodically to ensure no important emails are missed.

4. Enhanced Security: Blocking senders can enhance your email security by reducing the risk of phishing and other malicious emails reaching your inbox.

Additional Tools for Managing Junk Email

In addition to blocking senders, Outlook offers several other tools and features to help you manage junk email effectively:

1. Phishing Protection: Outlook includes built-in phishing protection that identifies and warns you about suspicious emails. If you receive a phishing email, you can report it directly from your inbox.

2. Junk Email Reporting: Outlook allows you to report junk email to Microsoft. By reporting spam, you help improve the overall filtering system, benefiting all users.

3. Junk Email Settings: Customize your junk email settings to suit your preferences. In the Junk E-mail Options dialog box, you can adjust the level of protection, specify trusted domains, and manage blocked and safe senders.

4. Third-Party Add-Ins: Consider using third-party add-ins and tools designed to enhance junk email management. These tools can offer additional filtering options and advanced features to keep your inbox clean.

Conclusion

Managing junk email is an essential part of maintaining an organized and efficient inbox. By blocking senders, you can significantly reduce the amount of spam you receive and improve your overall email experience. Remember to regularly review and update your blocked senders list, use additional filtering tools, and report any persistent spam to your email provider. With these strategies in place, you can enjoy a clutter-free inbox and focus on the emails that matter most.

10.1.2 Safe Senders List

The Safe Senders List in Outlook is a feature that allows users to specify which email addresses or domains should never be treated as junk mail. Adding trusted contacts to this list ensures that their emails will always land in your inbox, bypassing the junk email filter entirely. This feature is particularly useful for making sure you don't miss important emails from friends, family, or colleagues.

Why Use the Safe Senders List?

The primary reason for using the Safe Senders List is to avoid false positives, where legitimate emails are mistakenly marked as junk. By adding known and trusted email addresses to this list, you can ensure that important messages are not missed. This can be particularly critical in professional settings, where missing an email can lead to missed opportunities or important updates.

How to Add Contacts to the Safe Senders List

Adding contacts to the Safe Senders List in Outlook is a straightforward process. Here are the step-by-step instructions:

1. Open Outlook: Launch Outlook on your computer.

2. Navigate to Junk Email Options: Click on the "Home" tab on the ribbon at the top of the screen. In the "Delete" group, you'll find the "Junk" button. Click on it, and from the dropdown menu, select "Junk E-mail Options."

3. Access Safe Senders Tab: In the Junk E-mail Options dialog box, click on the "Safe Senders" tab.

4. Add New Safe Sender: To add a new email address or domain to the Safe Senders List, click on the "Add" button. A small dialog box will appear.

5. Enter Email Address or Domain: In the dialog box, enter the email address or domain you want to add. For example, if you want to ensure that emails from john.doe@example.com are never marked as junk, you would enter this email address. If you want to add an entire domain, you would enter @example.com.

6. Confirm and Add: Click "OK" to add the email address or domain to your Safe Senders List. You can repeat this process to add multiple addresses or domains.

7. Save Changes: Once you have added all the desired addresses and domains, click "Apply" and then "OK" to save your changes.

Managing the Safe Senders List

Over time, you may need to update your Safe Senders List by adding new contacts or removing old ones. Here's how you can manage your list:

1. Edit Existing Entries: To edit an existing entry, select the email address or domain in the Safe Senders tab and click on the "Edit" button. Make your changes and click "OK" to save.

2. Remove Entries: To remove an entry from the Safe Senders List, select the address or domain and click on the "Remove" button. Confirm the removal if prompted.

3. Importing and Exporting Safe Senders Lists: If you use multiple computers or need to share your Safe Senders List with others, you can import and export your list. Click on the "Import from File" or "Export to File" buttons and follow the prompts to complete the process.

Advanced Options for Safe Senders

Outlook provides additional options to fine-tune how the Safe Senders List operates:

1. Automatically Add People You Email: One useful feature is the option to automatically add people you email to the Safe Senders List. This can be enabled by checking the box labeled "Also trust e-mail from my Contacts" in the Safe Senders tab. This ensures that anyone you email will not be marked as junk, which is particularly useful for maintaining communication with new contacts.

2. Trust Emails from Your Contacts: Another option is to trust all emails from people in your Outlook Contacts. By enabling this feature, you can ensure that emails from your saved contacts are always delivered to your inbox.

Troubleshooting Safe Senders List Issues

While the Safe Senders List is a powerful tool, you may encounter some issues or need to troubleshoot specific problems:

1. Emails Still Going to Junk: If emails from addresses or domains on your Safe Senders List are still going to junk, check if there are any conflicting rules or settings. Ensure that the email addresses are entered correctly and not duplicated with different criteria.

2. Syncing Across Devices: If you use Outlook on multiple devices, ensure that your Safe Senders List is synchronized across all devices. You can do this by exporting the list from one device and importing it to others.

3. Regular Updates: Regularly review and update your Safe Senders List to reflect changes in your contacts and communication patterns. This will help maintain the effectiveness of your junk email management.

Best Practices for Using the Safe Senders List

To get the most out of the Safe Senders List, consider the following best practices:

1. Regularly Review Your List: Periodically review your Safe Senders List to ensure it includes all necessary contacts and domains. Remove any outdated or unnecessary entries to keep the list current and relevant.

2. Be Selective: Only add trusted and frequently contacted email addresses and domains to your Safe Senders List. Adding too many entries can reduce the effectiveness of your junk email filter.

3. Educate Your Contacts: Inform your contacts about adding your email address to their Safe Senders List. This can help ensure smooth communication and reduce the chances of your emails being marked as junk on their end.

Conclusion

The Safe Senders List is an essential tool in Outlook for managing junk email and ensuring that important messages are always delivered to your inbox. By understanding how to add, manage, and troubleshoot your Safe Senders List, you can significantly enhance your email experience. This proactive approach to email management helps maintain an organized and efficient inbox, allowing you to focus on your most important communications without the distraction of unwanted spam.

In the next section, we will explore how to use encryption in Outlook to secure your emails and protect sensitive information.

10.2 Using Encryption

10.2.1 Encrypting Emails

Email encryption in Outlook can be achieved through various methods. These methods include using S/MIME (Secure/Multipurpose Internet Mail Extensions) certificates and Office 365 Message Encryption. Each of these methods provides a different level of security and is suited to different needs. Let's explore these methods in detail.

Understanding Email Encryption

Before diving into the steps, it's important to understand what email encryption entails. When you send an email, it travels through various servers before reaching the recipient. During this journey, it can be intercepted and read by unauthorized parties. Encryption scrambles the content of the email, making it unreadable to anyone who does not have the decryption key.

S/MIME Certificates

S/MIME is a widely-used method for email encryption and digital signatures. It uses a pair of cryptographic keys - a public key for encrypting the email and a private key for decrypting it. Here's how to set up and use S/MIME certificates in Outlook:

1. Obtain an S/MIME Certificate:

   - You need to acquire an S/MIME certificate from a trusted Certificate Authority (CA). Some popular CAs include Comodo, Symantec, and GlobalSign. Follow the instructions provided by the CA to get your certificate.

2. Install the S/MIME Certificate:

   - Once you have the certificate, you need to install it on your computer. The CA will provide you with a file, usually with a .p7s or .pfx extension, along with a password.

3. Import the Certificate to Outlook:

- Open Outlook and go to the "File" menu.

- Select "Options" and then "Trust Center."

- Click on "Trust Center Settings" and then "Email Security."

- Under the "Digital IDs (Certificates)" section, click "Import/Export."

- Follow the prompts to import your S/MIME certificate. You will need to enter the password provided by the CA.

4. Configure Outlook to Use the S/MIME Certificate:

  - In the "Email Security" section, click on "Settings."

  - Choose your certificate under the "Signing Certificate" and "Encryption Certificate" sections.

  - Configure the security settings as per your requirement, including choosing the encryption algorithm.

5. Encrypt and Sign Emails:

  - When composing a new email, click on the "Options" tab.

  - In the "Permissions" group, click "Encrypt" and then choose "Encrypt with S/MIME."

  - You can also digitally sign your email by clicking "Sign" in the same group.

  - Complete your email and send it as usual.

Office 365 Message Encryption

If you are using Office 365, you can take advantage of Office 365 Message Encryption. This method is particularly useful for organizations as it integrates seamlessly with Office 365 services. Here's how to use it:

1. Enable Office 365 Message Encryption:

  - As an administrator, log in to the Office 365 Admin Center.

  - Go to the "Exchange Admin Center" and navigate to "Mail Flow."

- Select "Rules" and create a new rule.

- Name your rule and set the conditions under which the rule will apply. For instance, you can set it to apply to all outgoing emails.

- In the "Do the following" section, select "Modify the message security" and then "Apply Office 365 Message Encryption."

- Save your rule.

2. Encrypting Emails:

- Compose a new email in Outlook.

- Click on the "Options" tab.

- In the "Permissions" group, select "Encrypt."

- Choose the appropriate encryption option, such as "Encrypt-Only" or "Do Not Forward."

- Complete your email and send it as usual.

Best Practices for Email Encryption

1. Regularly Update Your Security Settings:

- Ensure that your encryption settings and certificates are up to date. Regular updates can protect you against new vulnerabilities and threats.

2. Educate Recipients:

- Make sure that the recipients of your encrypted emails understand how to decrypt and read them. This might involve providing instructions or support for installing and using S/MIME certificates.

3. Use Strong Passwords:

- For encrypted emails that require a password, always use strong, unique passwords. Avoid using easily guessable information.

4. Backup Your Encryption Keys:

- Losing your encryption keys can result in losing access to your encrypted emails. Ensure that you have a secure backup of your keys.

5. Monitor for Security Alerts:

  - Keep an eye on security alerts from your email provider and take immediate action if any unusual activity is detected.

Troubleshooting Common Issues

1. Problems with Certificate Installation:

  - Ensure that the certificate file is not corrupted and that you are entering the correct password. If issues persist, contact the CA for support.

2. Recipients Unable to Decrypt Emails:

  - Verify that the recipient has the appropriate software and has installed their S/MIME certificate correctly. Ensure that the public key has been shared securely.

3. Encryption Options Not Visible:

  - Make sure that the encryption feature is enabled in your version of Outlook. Check the settings under the "Trust Center" to ensure everything is configured correctly.

Conclusion

Encrypting your emails is an essential step in protecting your communication. By following the steps outlined in this section, you can ensure that your emails are secure and that sensitive information remains confidential. Whether you use S/MIME certificates or Office 365 Message Encryption, understanding and implementing email encryption in Outlook will significantly enhance your email security.

10.2.2 Managing Encryption Settings

In today's digital age, data security is of utmost importance. Encrypting emails ensures that your messages are secure and can only be read by the intended recipient. This section will guide you through managing encryption settings in Outlook, providing step-by-step instructions to help you enhance the security of your email communications.

Understanding Encryption Settings

Before diving into the practical steps, it's essential to understand what encryption settings are and why they are crucial. Encryption transforms your email content into an unreadable format for anyone except the recipient who has the decryption key. Outlook offers different types of encryption:

1. S/MIME Encryption: Secure/Multipurpose Internet Mail Extensions (S/MIME) is a widely used method for encrypting and signing emails. It requires a digital certificate, which acts as a digital ID for both encryption and digital signatures.

2. Office 365 Message Encryption: This is a feature available to Office 365 subscribers that allows you to send encrypted emails to anyone, whether they use Outlook or another email service.

Setting Up S/MIME Encryption

To use S/MIME encryption, follow these steps:

1. Obtain a Digital Certificate:

   - Purchase a digital certificate from a trusted certificate authority (CA) such as Comodo, DigiCert, or GlobalSign.

   - Follow the instructions provided by the CA to download and install the certificate on your computer.

2. Install the Certificate in Outlook:

   - Open Outlook and go to `File` > `Options` > `Trust Center`.

   - Click on `Trust Center Settings`.

   - Select `Email Security`.

- In the `Encrypted Email` section, click on `Settings`.

- Choose the certificate you installed from the `Certificate and Algorithms` section.

3. Encrypting an Email:

   - Create a new email message.

   - Click on `Options` in the ribbon.

   - In the `Permissions` group, click on `Encrypt`.

   - Select `Encrypt with S/MIME`.

   - Compose your email and send it.

Managing Office 365 Message Encryption

For Office 365 subscribers, managing encryption settings is straightforward:

1. Encrypting an Email:

   - Create a new email message.

   - Click on `Options` in the ribbon.

   - In the `Permissions` group, click on `Encrypt`.

   - Choose the appropriate encryption option such as `Encrypt-Only` or `Do Not Forward`.

   - Compose your email and send it.

2. Managing Encrypted Messages:

   - You can manage encrypted messages from the `Sent Items` folder.

   - Double-click on the sent encrypted message to open it.

   - Use the `Options` tab to change permissions or resend the encrypted message.

Configuring Encryption Policies

Encryption policies determine how your emails are encrypted and who can access them. These policies can be configured by your IT administrator if you're using a business account. However, personal users can also set up basic policies:

1. Accessing Encryption Policies:

   - Go to `File` > `Options` > `Trust Center`.

   - Click on `Trust Center Settings`.

   - Select `Email Security`.

2. Setting Default Encryption Options:

   - In the `Encrypted Email` section, you can set your default encryption and signing options.

   - Select the `Encrypt contents and attachments for outgoing messages` checkbox to ensure all outgoing emails are encrypted by default.

   - Choose the default certificate for signing and encryption from the `Certificates and Algorithms` section.

3. Managing Encrypted Email Rules:

   - You can create rules to automatically encrypt emails based on specific criteria.

   - Go to `File` > `Manage Rules & Alerts`.

   - Click on `New Rule` and select a template such as `Apply rule on messages I send`.

   - Specify the conditions under which the rule should apply, such as emails sent to a particular recipient or containing specific keywords.

   - In the `Actions` section, select `encrypt the message with S/MIME` or `apply Office 365 Message Encryption`.

Troubleshooting Encryption Issues

Even with the proper setup, you might encounter issues with email encryption. Here are some common problems and solutions:

1. Certificate Not Found:

   - Ensure the digital certificate is correctly installed on your computer.

   - Verify that Outlook is configured to use the correct certificate by checking `File` > `Options` > `Trust Center` > `Trust Center Settings` > `Email Security`.

2. Recipient Cannot Decrypt the Message:

   - Make sure the recipient has shared their public encryption key with you.

   - Verify that the recipient's email client supports S/MIME encryption.

   - If using Office 365 Message Encryption, ensure the recipient follows the instructions in the encrypted email to read the message.

3. Error Messages When Sending Encrypted Emails:

   - Check your internet connection and try again.

   - Verify that your email account settings are correct.

   - If the problem persists, contact your email service provider or IT administrator for further assistance.

Best Practices for Email Encryption

To ensure the highest level of security for your encrypted emails, follow these best practices:

1. Regularly Update Your Digital Certificates:

   - Digital certificates typically have an expiration date. Ensure you renew your certificate before it expires to avoid disruptions in your email encryption.

2. Verify Recipient's Encryption Capability:

   - Before sending encrypted emails, confirm that the recipient can decrypt them. For S/MIME encryption, exchange public keys with your contacts.

3. Secure Your Private Key:

- The private key associated with your digital certificate should be stored securely. Do not share it with anyone and ensure your computer is protected with strong passwords and security measures.

4. Educate Recipients:

- If your recipients are not familiar with encrypted emails, provide them with instructions on how to open and read encrypted messages. This is especially important for Office 365 Message Encryption.

5. Use Encryption Consistently:

- Make encryption a standard practice for all sensitive communications. Consistent use of encryption helps protect your data and reduces the risk of information leakage.

By managing your encryption settings effectively, you can significantly enhance the security of your email communications in Outlook. Whether you are using S/MIME or Office 365 Message Encryption, following the steps outlined in this section will help you protect your sensitive information and ensure that your emails are only read by the intended recipients.

10.3 Protecting Your Outlook Account

Protecting your Outlook account is crucial to ensure that your personal and professional information remains secure. One of the fundamental steps in safeguarding your account is setting a strong password. A robust password serves as the first line of defense against unauthorized access. This section will guide you through the importance of strong passwords, how to create them, and best practices for managing them.

10.3.1 Setting Strong Passwords

A strong password is essential for protecting your Outlook account from hackers and unauthorized users. Weak passwords are easy targets for cybercriminals who use various techniques to gain access to accounts. Here, we will explore the characteristics of strong passwords, provide guidelines on creating them, and discuss methods for maintaining password security.

1. Importance of Strong Passwords

The significance of a strong password cannot be overstated. With the increasing prevalence of cyber threats, a robust password acts as a critical barrier that prevents unauthorized individuals from accessing your account. Here are a few reasons why strong passwords are essential:

- Protection from Brute Force Attacks: Hackers often use automated tools to guess passwords by trying numerous combinations. A strong password, with its complexity and length, makes it significantly harder for these tools to succeed.

- Security of Personal Information: Your Outlook account likely contains sensitive information, including emails, contacts, and calendar events. A strong password ensures that this information remains confidential.

- Prevention of Unauthorized Access: By setting a strong password, you reduce the risk of someone gaining unauthorized access to your account and misusing your data.

2. Characteristics of Strong Passwords

A strong password typically has the following characteristics:

- Length: The longer the password, the harder it is to crack. Aim for a minimum of 12 characters.

- Complexity: A mix of uppercase and lowercase letters, numbers, and special characters increases the difficulty of guessing the password.

- Unpredictability: Avoid common words, phrases, or easily guessable patterns like "password123" or "qwerty."

- Uniqueness: Use a different password for each of your accounts to prevent a breach in one account from compromising others.

3. Guidelines for Creating Strong Passwords

Creating a strong password involves following certain guidelines to ensure it meets the necessary security criteria. Here are some tips to help you generate a robust password:

- Combine Different Character Types: Use a combination of uppercase letters, lowercase letters, numbers, and special characters. For example, a password like "S3cur3P@ssw0rd!" is much stronger than "securepassword."

- Avoid Common Passwords: Do not use easily guessable passwords such as "password," "123456," or "admin." These are among the first that hackers will try.

- Use Passphrases: Consider using a passphrase, which is a series of words or a sentence that is easy for you to remember but difficult for others to guess. For example, "T!mGrewAB!gT@llTreeIn2024" is a strong passphrase.

- Include Unpredictable Elements: Avoid using personal information such as your name, birthdate, or pet's name, as these can be easily guessed by someone who knows you or can find the information online.

- Use Password Generators: If you struggle to come up with strong passwords, use an online password generator to create complex and random passwords.

4. Best Practices for Managing Passwords

Creating a strong password is just the first step; managing your passwords properly is equally important to ensure ongoing security. Here are some best practices for managing your passwords:

- Do Not Reuse Passwords: Each of your accounts should have a unique password. Reusing passwords across multiple sites increases the risk of a security breach.

- Change Passwords Regularly: Periodically update your passwords to reduce the risk of them being compromised over time.

- Use a Password Manager: Password managers can help you generate, store, and manage strong passwords securely. They can also auto-fill login forms, making it easier to use complex passwords without having to remember them.

- Enable Two-Factor Authentication: Whenever possible, enable two-factor authentication (2FA) for an added layer of security. This ensures that even if someone obtains your password, they will still need a second form of verification to access your account.

5. How to Change Your Outlook Password

Changing your Outlook password is a straightforward process. Follow these steps to update your password:

1. Sign in to Your Microsoft Account:

  - Go to the Microsoft account sign-in page and enter your current credentials.

2. Access Security Settings:

  - Navigate to the "Security" section of your account settings.

3. Change Your Password:

  - Select the option to change your password. You may be asked to verify your identity through a security code sent to your email or phone.

4. Enter a New Password:

- Follow the guidelines for creating a strong password and enter your new password. Confirm the new password by entering it again.

5. Save Changes:

- Save your changes and ensure that your new password is updated across all devices and apps where you use your Outlook account.

6. Tips for Remembering Strong Passwords

Remembering strong passwords can be challenging, especially if you follow the best practice of using unique passwords for each account. Here are some tips to help you remember your passwords:

- Use Mnemonics: Create a memorable phrase or sentence and use the first letter of each word, combined with numbers and special characters. For example, "My favorite vacation was in Paris in 2019!" could become "Mfvwip@2019!"

- Password Manager: As mentioned earlier, using a password manager can significantly reduce the burden of remembering multiple strong passwords.

- Write It Down (Carefully): If you must write down your passwords, ensure they are stored in a secure and private place, away from prying eyes.

7. Common Mistakes to Avoid

When setting and managing passwords, avoid these common mistakes to maintain optimal security:

- Using Simple and Short Passwords: Short and simple passwords are easy targets for hackers.

- Sharing Passwords: Never share your passwords with others. If you need to grant access, consider using shared access features or temporary passwords.

- Ignoring Password Updates: Regularly updating your passwords helps to prevent long-term vulnerabilities.

- Relying on Personal Information: Avoid using easily accessible personal information in your passwords, as this can be easily guessed or discovered.

8. Conclusion

Setting a strong password is a crucial step in protecting your Outlook account. By following the guidelines and best practices outlined in this section, you can significantly enhance the security of your account and safeguard your personal and professional information. Remember, a strong password is your first line of defense against cyber threats, and maintaining good password hygiene is essential for ongoing account security.

10.3.2 Enabling Two-Factor Authentication

Two-Factor Authentication (2FA) adds an additional layer of security to your Outlook account by requiring not only your password but also a second form of verification. This could be a code sent to your mobile phone or generated by an authenticator app. Here's how to enable 2FA for your Outlook account:

What is Two-Factor Authentication?

Two-Factor Authentication (2FA) is a security process in which users provide two different authentication factors to verify their identity. This method adds an extra layer of security to your accounts, as it requires both something you know (your password) and something you have (a second factor like a phone or an app).

Benefits of Enabling Two-Factor Authentication

1. Enhanced Security: Even if someone knows your password, they would still need the second factor to access your account.

2. Protection Against Phishing: 2FA can help protect your account from phishing attacks, as attackers would need more than just your password.

3. Increased Account Safety: Provides peace of mind knowing that your account has an additional layer of protection.

Steps to Enable Two-Factor Authentication for Outlook

Step 1: Sign in to Your Microsoft Account

1. Open a web browser and go to the Microsoft account sign-in page.

2. Enter your email address and password to sign in.

Step 2: Access Security Settings

1. Once signed in, go to the top navigation bar and click on your profile picture or initials.

2. From the drop-down menu, select "My Microsoft account".

3. In the Microsoft account dashboard, click on the "Security" tab.

Step 3: Set Up Two-Factor Authentication

1. Under the Security basics page, find the section titled "More security options" and click on it.

2. In the More security options section, locate "Two-step verification" and click on "Set up two-step verification".

3. Follow the on-screen instructions, which will guide you through setting up 2FA. This typically involves choosing how you want to receive your second factor: via phone call, text message, or an authenticator app.

Step 4: Choosing Your Verification Method

1. Phone Call or Text Message:

   - If you choose a phone call or text message, you will be prompted to enter your phone number.

   - Microsoft will send you a verification code to this number.

   - Enter the verification code on the website to verify your phone number.

2. Authenticator App:

  - Download an authenticator app, such as Microsoft Authenticator, Google Authenticator, or Authy, on your mobile device.

  - In the 2FA setup process, choose the option to use an app.

  - Open the app on your phone and scan the QR code displayed on the Microsoft website.

  - The app will generate a code that you need to enter on the website to verify the setup.

Step 5: Finalizing the Setup

1. After choosing and verifying your second factor, you will be asked to review your 2FA settings.

2. Microsoft will provide you with recovery codes. Important: Save these recovery codes in a safe place. They can be used to access your account if you lose access to your second factor.

3. Confirm the setup and complete the process.

Managing Your Two-Factor Authentication Settings

After setting up 2FA, you might need to manage your settings occasionally. Here's how you can do it:

1. Updating Your Phone Number:

  - If you change your phone number, go to the Security settings in your Microsoft account.

  - Under "Update your phone numbers used for account security", add your new phone number and remove the old one.

2. Switching Authenticator Apps:

  - If you want to switch to a different authenticator app, first add the new app using the same steps you followed initially.

  - After verifying the new app, remove the old one from your 2FA settings.

3. Generating New Recovery Codes:

- If you think your recovery codes have been compromised, you can generate new ones from the 2FA setup page.

Troubleshooting Common Issues with Two-Factor Authentication

1. Not Receiving Verification Codes:

   - Ensure your phone number is entered correctly and that you have good network coverage.

   - Check for any message or call blocking settings on your phone.

2. Lost Access to Second Factor:

   - Use the recovery codes provided during the setup to regain access to your account.

   - Contact Microsoft support if you are unable to use recovery codes.

3. Authenticator App Not Working:

   - Ensure the time on your phone is set to automatic. Incorrect time settings can cause issues with code generation.

   - Re-sync the app by scanning the QR code again from your Microsoft account settings.

Best Practices for Maintaining Account Security

1. Regularly Update Your Password: Change your password periodically and ensure it is strong and unique.

2. Monitor Account Activity: Regularly check your account activity for any suspicious behavior.

3. Use Different Passwords for Different Accounts: Avoid using the same password across multiple sites to reduce the risk of a single point of failure.

4. Enable Notifications for Account Activity: Set up alerts for any unusual sign-in attempts or changes to your account settings.

By enabling Two-Factor Authentication and following these best practices, you significantly enhance the security of your Outlook account, protecting it from unauthorized access and potential cyber threats. With 2FA, you can rest assured that your personal and professional information remains safe and secure.

CHAPTER XI
Troubleshooting and Support

11.1 Common Issues and Solutions

11.1.1 Email Sending and Receiving Problems

Email communication is a crucial part of modern business and personal communication, and issues with sending or receiving emails can cause significant disruptions. This section will address common problems users might encounter while using Outlook and provide comprehensive solutions to resolve these issues effectively.

Common Issues with Sending Emails

1. Email Stuck in Outbox: One of the most common issues is when emails get stuck in the Outbox and are not sent. This can be due to several reasons:

   - Network Issues: If your internet connection is unstable or lost, emails may fail to send. Ensure you have a stable internet connection.

   - Large Attachments: Emails with large attachments can sometimes fail to send. Check the size of your attachments and consider reducing them or using a file-sharing service.

   - Outlook Offline Mode: Sometimes, Outlook might be set to work offline. Ensure that Outlook is in online mode by clicking on the "Send/Receive" tab and checking the "Work Offline" button.

2. Incorrect Email Address: If the recipient's email address is entered incorrectly, the email will not be sent. Double-check the email addresses for typos or errors.

3. Authentication Issues: If Outlook is not properly authenticated with your email server, it may fail to send emails.

- Check Account Settings: Go to File > Account Settings > Account Settings. Select your email account and click on "Change." Verify that your username, password, and server settings are correct.

- Re-enter Credentials: Sometimes, simply re-entering your password can resolve authentication issues.

4. Outdated Outlook Version: Ensure that you are using the latest version of Outlook. Outdated software can sometimes cause compatibility issues.

- Update Outlook: Go to File > Office Account > Update Options and select "Update Now" to ensure you have the latest updates installed.

Common Issues with Receiving Emails

1. Network Issues: Similar to sending emails, receiving emails also requires a stable internet connection. Ensure your internet connection is working properly.

2. Email Filter Settings: Sometimes, incoming emails might be filtered into the spam or junk folder.

- Check Spam/Junk Folder: Navigate to your spam or junk folder to see if any legitimate emails have been filtered there.

- Adjust Filter Settings: If you find legitimate emails in the spam/junk folder, adjust your filter settings to ensure these emails are delivered to your inbox in the future.

3. Mailbox Full: If your mailbox storage is full, new emails will not be received.

- Delete Unnecessary Emails: Clear out old or unnecessary emails from your inbox, sent items, and trash folders.

- Archive Emails: Consider archiving older emails to free up space in your mailbox.

4. Server Issues: Sometimes, the issue might be on the email server side.

- Check Server Status: Contact your email service provider to check if there are any ongoing server issues.

- Server Settings: Ensure that your incoming mail server settings are correct. Go to File > Account Settings > Account Settings, select your email account, and click on "Change." Verify the server settings.

Troubleshooting Steps

1. Restart Outlook: Sometimes, simply restarting Outlook can resolve many issues. Close Outlook and reopen it to see if the problem persists.

2. Check for Updates: Ensure that both your operating system and Outlook are up to date. Go to File > Office Account > Update Options and select "Update Now."

3. Run the Inbox Repair Tool: Outlook provides an Inbox Repair Tool (SCANPST.EXE) to fix corrupted files.

   - Locate SCANPST.EXE: The location of this tool varies depending on your Outlook version. Generally, it can be found in the Office installation folder.

   - Run the Tool: Open SCANPST.EXE and follow the on-screen instructions to scan and repair your PST file.

4. Create a New Profile: Sometimes, creating a new Outlook profile can resolve persistent issues.

   - Open Control Panel: Navigate to Control Panel and select "Mail."

   - Show Profiles: Click on "Show Profiles" and then "Add" to create a new profile.

   - Configure Email Account: Follow the instructions to set up your email account in the new profile.

5. Disable Add-Ins: Some add-ins can interfere with email sending and receiving.

   - Open Outlook in Safe Mode: Hold down the Ctrl key while opening Outlook to start it in Safe Mode.

   - Disable Add-Ins: Go to File > Options > Add-Ins. Click on "Go" next to Manage COM Add-ins and uncheck all add-ins. Restart Outlook to see if the issue is resolved.

6. Check Firewall and Antivirus Settings: Sometimes, firewall or antivirus settings can block email communication.

   - Temporarily Disable Antivirus: Temporarily disable your antivirus program to see if it resolves the issue.

   - Adjust Firewall Settings: Ensure that Outlook is allowed through your firewall settings.

Preventive Measures

1. Regular Maintenance: Regularly clean up your mailbox, archive old emails, and ensure your mailbox is not nearing its storage limit.

2. Backup Emails: Regularly back up your emails to avoid data loss in case of issues.

3. Update Software: Keep your operating system, Outlook, and all related software up to date to ensure compatibility and security.

4. Use Strong Passwords: Ensure your email account is protected with a strong password and enable two-factor authentication if available.

By following these steps and preventive measures, users can effectively troubleshoot and resolve common email sending and receiving problems in Outlook. Regular maintenance and staying updated with the latest software versions can also help prevent these issues from occurring in the first place.

11.1.2 Calendar Sync Issues

One of the common challenges faced by Outlook users is calendar synchronization issues. These problems can manifest in various ways, such as missing events, duplicate entries, or discrepancies between devices. Effective calendar synchronization is crucial for maintaining an accurate schedule, especially for users who rely on multiple devices for work and personal tasks. This section will delve into the potential causes of calendar sync issues and provide step-by-step solutions to resolve them.

Understanding Calendar Sync Issues

Calendar synchronization issues can arise from several factors:

- Internet Connectivity: Poor or intermittent internet connections can disrupt the sync process.

- Server Issues: Problems with the email server or the Exchange server can hinder synchronization.

- Software Bugs: Glitches in the Outlook application or the operating system can affect calendar sync.

- Configuration Errors: Incorrect account settings or sync settings can prevent proper synchronization.

- Third-Party Applications: Conflicts with other calendar applications or add-ins can cause sync issues.

Troubleshooting Calendar Sync Issues

To address calendar sync issues, follow these comprehensive steps:

1. Check Internet Connectivity

  - Ensure that your device is connected to the internet. A stable and robust connection is essential for seamless synchronization.

  - Test your internet connection by opening a web browser and navigating to a few websites. If the websites load correctly, your internet connection is likely not the issue.

2. Verify Server Status

  - Sometimes, the issue might be on the server side. Check the status of your email server or the Exchange server.

  - You can visit the service provider's status page (e.g., Office 365 Service Health) to see if there are any ongoing outages or maintenance activities.

3. Update Outlook and Operating System

  - Ensure that you have the latest version of Outlook installed. Software updates often include bug fixes that can resolve sync issues.

  - Similarly, make sure your operating system is up-to-date. Operating system updates can also address underlying issues that affect applications.

4. Review Account Settings

  - Open Outlook and navigate to `File > Account Settings > Account Settings`.

- Select your email account and click `Change`. Verify that the server settings are correct. You can compare these settings with those provided by your email service provider.

- Ensure that the `Use Cached Exchange Mode` checkbox is selected if you are using an Exchange account. This setting helps in maintaining an offline copy of your mailbox and calendar.

5. Check Sync Settings

   - Go to `File > Options > Advanced`.

   - Scroll down to the `Send and receive` section and click `Send/Receive...`.

   - Ensure that the `Include this group in send/receive (F9)` checkbox is checked for your account.

   - Review the `Download options` to ensure that `Download full items including attachments for subscribed folders` is selected.

6. Reset Calendar View

   - Sometimes, the calendar view might be corrupted, causing sync issues. Resetting the view can help.

   - In Outlook, go to `View > Change View > Manage Views`.

   - Select `Reset View` to revert the calendar view to its default settings.

7. Clear the Offline Items

   - If your calendar is not syncing properly, clearing the offline items and forcing a resync can help.

   - Navigate to `File > Account Settings > Account Settings`.

   - Select your account, click `Change`, and then `More Settings`.

   - Go to the `Advanced` tab and click `Outlook Data File Settings`.

   - Click `Disable Offline Use`, then `Yes`, and finally, `OK`. This action will clear the offline data.

   - Re-enable offline use by following the same steps and clicking `Enable Offline Use`.

8. Repair Outlook Data File

- Corrupted data files can cause synchronization issues. Use the built-in repair tool to fix these files.

- Close Outlook and open the `Inbox Repair Tool` (SCANPST.EXE). This tool is located in the Outlook installation directory.

- Select your Outlook data file (PST) and click `Start` to begin the repair process. Follow the on-screen instructions to complete the repair.

9. Disable Conflicting Add-Ins

  - Third-party add-ins can interfere with Outlook's synchronization processes.

  - Go to `File > Options > Add-ins`.

  - At the bottom of the window, select `COM Add-ins` from the `Manage` dropdown and click `Go`.

  - Uncheck any add-ins that you do not recognize or do not need, and then click `OK`.

  - Restart Outlook to see if the sync issues are resolved.

10. Recreate Your Outlook Profile

  - If none of the above solutions work, recreating your Outlook profile can help.

  - Go to `Control Panel > Mail > Show Profiles`.

  - Click `Add` to create a new profile. Follow the prompts to set up your email account in the new profile.

  - Once the new profile is created, select `Prompt for a profile to be used` and launch Outlook using the new profile.

  - Check if the calendar sync issues are resolved. If they are, you can delete the old profile.

Additional Tips

- Sync Frequency: Ensure that your calendar sync frequency is set appropriately. Go to `Send/Receive Groups > Define Send/Receive Groups` and adjust the sync frequency to a lower interval if necessary.

- Mobile Device Sync: If you are experiencing sync issues on a mobile device, try removing and re-adding your email account. Ensure that the sync settings on your mobile device are configured correctly.

- Outlook Web App: Check if your calendar is syncing correctly on the Outlook Web App (OWA). If the web app shows accurate data, the issue might be with the Outlook client on your device.

- Support Forums and Communities: Utilize online forums and communities for additional support. Websites like Microsoft's support community can provide valuable insights and solutions from other users experiencing similar issues.

Seeking Professional Help

If you continue to experience calendar sync issues despite following these troubleshooting steps, it might be time to seek professional assistance. Contact your IT department or Microsoft Support for further help. They can provide advanced diagnostics and solutions tailored to your specific setup and environment.

By following these detailed troubleshooting steps, you can effectively address and resolve most calendar sync issues in Outlook, ensuring that your schedule remains accurate and up-to-date across all your devices.

11.2 Getting Help and Support

11.2.1 Using the Help Feature

In this section, we'll delve into the comprehensive help features available in Microsoft Outlook that can assist you in navigating through any issues you might encounter. Utilizing the help feature effectively can save time and improve your overall experience with the application.

Understanding the Help Feature

Microsoft Outlook comes equipped with a built-in help system designed to provide users with immediate assistance on a wide range of topics. This feature is especially useful for beginners who might not be familiar with all the functionalities Outlook has to offer. The help system is integrated directly into the application, making it accessible at any time without needing to leave Outlook.

Accessing the Help Feature

To access the help feature in Outlook, you can use several methods:

1. Help Button: Located in the ribbon, usually marked with a question mark or labeled as "Help." Clicking this button opens the help pane.

2. F1 Key: Pressing the F1 key on your keyboard is a quick shortcut to open the help pane.

3. Tell Me What You Want to Do: This feature, found at the top of the ribbon, allows you to type in a keyword or question. It provides immediate links to help articles or suggests actions directly within Outlook.

Navigating the Help Pane

Once you have accessed the help feature, the help pane will appear on the right side of the Outlook window. This pane is your gateway to a wealth of information and support. Here are some key components you will find in the help pane:

1. Search Bar: At the top of the help pane, you will find a search bar where you can type in keywords or questions related to the issue you are facing. The search function is highly intuitive and will provide you with relevant articles, guides, and tips.

2. Topics and Categories: The help pane categorizes help topics for easier navigation. You can browse through categories such as "Email," "Calendar," "People," "Tasks," and more to find the specific help you need.

3. Popular Searches: This section lists commonly searched topics, providing quick access to frequently asked questions and common issues.

Utilizing Search Functionality

The search functionality within the help pane is a powerful tool that can assist you in finding specific information quickly. Here are some tips for making the most out of the search feature:

1. Use Specific Keywords: When searching for help, use specific keywords related to your issue. For example, if you are having trouble with email attachments, type "email attachments" rather than a general term like "email."

2. Ask Questions: You can type full questions into the search bar, such as "How do I create a new email folder?" The help system is designed to understand natural language queries and will provide relevant results.

3. Explore Suggested Topics: As you type in the search bar, the help pane will suggest topics and articles. Explore these suggestions to find the most relevant help articles.

Reading Help Articles

Once you have found a help article that seems relevant to your issue, click on it to open it in the help pane. Help articles in Outlook are designed to be user-friendly and comprehensive. Here are some features you will find in help articles:

1. Step-by-Step Instructions: Many help articles provide detailed, step-by-step instructions on how to perform a task or resolve an issue. These instructions are often accompanied by screenshots or diagrams to make them easier to follow.

2. Related Topics: At the end of help articles, you will find links to related topics that might be useful. These links can provide additional context or guide you to further reading on a particular subject.

3. Printable Version: Some help articles offer a printable version, which can be useful if you prefer to have a hard copy of the instructions.

Interactive Guides and Videos

In addition to traditional help articles, Outlook's help feature also includes interactive guides and video tutorials. These resources can be particularly helpful for visual learners. Here are some types of interactive content you might find:

1. Video Tutorials: Short, instructional videos that demonstrate how to perform specific tasks in Outlook. These videos often include voice-over explanations and on-screen annotations to guide you through the process.

2. Interactive Simulations: Step-by-step interactive guides that simulate the actions you need to take within the Outlook interface. These simulations allow you to practice tasks in a controlled environment without affecting your actual data.

3. Webinars and Training Sessions: Links to live or recorded webinars and training sessions conducted by Outlook experts. These sessions can provide in-depth knowledge on various aspects of Outlook.

Tips and Tricks

The help feature also includes a section dedicated to tips and tricks. These articles offer insights into lesser-known features and shortcuts that can enhance your productivity. Examples include keyboard shortcuts, customization options, and advanced settings.

Using the "Tell Me What You Want to Do" Feature

One of the most innovative aspects of Outlook's help system is the "Tell Me What You Want to Do" feature. This tool, found at the top of the ribbon, allows you to type in tasks or questions in plain language. Here's how to use it effectively:

1. Typing Tasks: Enter the task you want to perform, such as "create a new folder" or "schedule a meeting." The feature will provide direct links to the relevant commands or settings within Outlook.

2. Getting Help: If you type a question, such as "How do I add an attachment?", the feature will offer links to help articles that address your query.

3. Actionable Suggestions: In many cases, the feature will provide actionable suggestions that you can click on directly, allowing you to perform tasks without navigating through multiple menus.

Feedback and User Contributions

Outlook's help system is continually updated based on user feedback and contributions. Here's how you can contribute to improving the help feature:

1. Providing Feedback: At the bottom of most help articles, you will find an option to provide feedback. You can rate the article and leave comments on whether it was helpful or suggest improvements.

2. Suggesting New Topics: If you encounter an issue that is not covered in the help system, you can suggest new topics or questions for future inclusion. This helps Microsoft improve the help resources based on real user experiences.

Offline Help

For situations where you might not have internet access, Outlook also offers offline help resources. Here's how to access and use offline help:

1. Downloading Help Files: You can download help files from the Outlook website or within the application to ensure you have access to essential information even when offline.

2. Accessing Offline Help: Once downloaded, you can access offline help through the same help feature interface. The content will be stored locally on your device, allowing you to search and read help articles without an internet connection.

Conclusion

Using the help feature in Outlook is an invaluable resource for beginners and experienced users alike. By familiarizing yourself with how to access and navigate the help system, you can resolve issues more efficiently and enhance your overall experience with Outlook. Whether you are looking for step-by-step instructions, troubleshooting tips, or advanced techniques, the help feature is designed to provide you with the information you need right at your fingertips.

11.2.2 Contacting Support

When you encounter issues that you cannot resolve using the built-in help feature, it may be necessary to contact Microsoft Support for further assistance. Microsoft offers several avenues for getting help with Outlook, ranging from online resources to direct contact with support representatives. Here's how to make the most out of these support options:

1. Online Support and Resources

  - Microsoft Support Website: The first place to check for help is the Microsoft Support website. It contains a vast amount of information, including articles, tutorials, FAQs, and troubleshooting guides that cover almost every aspect of Outlook.

   - Accessing the Support Website: Navigate to [support.microsoft.com] (https://support.microsoft.com) and select Outlook from the list of products. You can use the search bar to find specific issues or browse through various topics.

   - Knowledge Base: The knowledge base is an extensive collection of articles written by Microsoft experts. It is a valuable resource for finding solutions to both common and obscure problems.

- Community Forums: The Microsoft Community Forums are another excellent resource. Here, you can ask questions and get answers from other Outlook users as well as Microsoft MVPs (Most Valuable Professionals) who are highly knowledgeable about the product.

2. Contacting Microsoft Support

- Support via Email: If you prefer not to speak with a support representative directly, you can reach out to Microsoft Support via email. This method allows you to describe your issue in detail and receive a written response that you can refer back to if needed.

- How to Email Support: To contact support via email, go to the Microsoft Support website, select Outlook, and look for the "Contact Us" option. Follow the prompts to describe your issue and submit your request.

- Live Chat Support: For more immediate assistance, live chat is a convenient option. It allows you to interact with a support representative in real-time via text chat.

- Accessing Live Chat: On the Microsoft Support website, select Outlook, then navigate to the "Contact Us" section. Choose the live chat option and you will be connected to a representative who can help with your issue.

- Phone Support: Speaking directly to a support representative over the phone can be the quickest way to resolve more complex issues.

- Finding the Support Number: The phone support number varies by region. On the Microsoft Support website, select Outlook and navigate to the "Contact Us" section. Here, you will find the appropriate phone number for your region.

- What to Expect: When you call, you will typically be asked to provide some basic information about your issue. Be prepared to describe the problem clearly and provide any error messages you may have received. The support representative will guide you through troubleshooting steps over the phone.

- In-App Support: Some versions of Outlook, particularly those included with Office 365, offer in-app support options. This feature allows you to get help without leaving the application.

- Accessing In-App Support: Look for a help or support option within the Outlook application. This might be found under the "Help" menu or as a support button in the ribbon.

3. Premium Support Options

- Microsoft 365 Subscription Benefits: If you have a Microsoft 365 subscription, you may be eligible for additional support options. These can include priority access to support representatives and more in-depth assistance.

- Accessing Premium Support: To access premium support options, sign in to your Microsoft 365 account and go to the support section. Here, you will see the additional support options available to you based on your subscription level.

- Microsoft Premier Support: For businesses and enterprises, Microsoft offers Premier Support services. This is a paid service that provides comprehensive support, including proactive services to help prevent issues, and dedicated account management.

- Premier Support Features: Services include on-site support, dedicated support engineers, and training for your IT staff to better manage and support Outlook and other Microsoft products.

- How to Enroll: To find out more about Premier Support and enroll, visit the Microsoft Services website or contact a Microsoft representative for more information.

4. Preparing for a Support Call

- Gathering Information: Before contacting support, gather all relevant information about your issue. This includes error messages, steps you have already taken to try to resolve the problem, and any relevant account information.

- Taking Screenshots: If possible, take screenshots of the issue and any error messages. These can be very helpful for the support representative in diagnosing the problem.

- Testing Steps: Be prepared to follow troubleshooting steps during the call. This might include changing settings, running diagnostics, or performing specific actions within Outlook.

5. Escalating Your Issue

- When to Escalate: If the initial support representative cannot resolve your issue, you may need to request escalation to a higher-level support team. This is especially true for complex or persistent problems.

- How to Escalate: Politely ask the support representative if it is possible to escalate your issue. Provide any additional details that may help in understanding why the issue needs further attention.

- Following Up: If your issue is escalated, make sure to get a case number or reference number. This will make it easier to follow up on the status of your issue if needed.

6. Support for Businesses

- Business Support Plans: Microsoft offers specialized support plans for businesses, including Microsoft 365 Business and Enterprise plans. These plans often include additional support features tailored to business needs.

- Features: Enhanced support options may include faster response times, dedicated support teams, and additional resources for IT administrators.

- Accessing Business Support: Business users can access support through the Microsoft 365 admin center or by contacting their dedicated account manager if they have one.

- Third-Party Support Providers: In addition to Microsoft's support services, there are also third-party providers that specialize in supporting Outlook and other Microsoft products. These providers can offer personalized support, training, and consulting services.

- Choosing a Provider: When selecting a third-party support provider, look for those with a strong track record, good customer reviews, and expertise in Outlook and Microsoft 365 products.

- Contracting Services: Many third-party providers offer support contracts that can include regular maintenance, on-call support, and proactive monitoring to prevent issues.

7. Self-Help Resources

- Outlook Help Center: The Outlook Help Center on the Microsoft website is a comprehensive resource for learning about Outlook features and troubleshooting common problems.

- Navigating the Help Center: Use the search bar to quickly find articles related to your issue, or browse through categories to learn more about specific features.

- Online Tutorials and Courses: There are many online platforms that offer tutorials and courses on using Outlook. Websites like LinkedIn Learning, Udemy, and Coursera provide in-depth lessons that can help you become more proficient in using Outlook.

- Selecting a Course: Look for courses that match your skill level and cover the specific features or issues you are interested in. Many platforms offer user reviews and ratings to help you choose the best course.

- YouTube and Blogs: Many tech enthusiasts and experts share their knowledge about Outlook through YouTube channels and blogs. These resources can provide quick tips, troubleshooting advice, and detailed walkthroughs of Outlook features.

- Finding Quality Content: Search for reputable channels and blogs with a focus on Microsoft products and good subscriber or reader engagement. Pay attention to the quality of the content and whether it is regularly updated.

CHAPTER XII
Conclusion

12.1 Summary of Key Points

In this comprehensive guide, we have explored the fundamental aspects of using Microsoft Outlook effectively. Let's summarize the key points covered in each chapter to reinforce your understanding and ensure you are well-equipped to navigate Outlook with confidence.

Chapter 1: Introduction to Outlook

We began with an introduction to Outlook, explaining its role as a powerful email and personal information management tool. Outlook is part of the Microsoft Office suite and offers a wide range of features that go beyond simple email handling. These include calendar management, task tracking, contact management, and more.

Key Takeaways:

- Understanding Outlook: Outlook is a multifaceted tool designed to streamline communication and organization.

- Benefits of Outlook: It enhances productivity through efficient email management, calendar scheduling, and integrated task and contact management.

- Setting Up Outlook: Initial setup involves creating an account and configuring basic settings to tailor the application to your needs.

Chapter 2: Getting Started with Outlook

In this chapter, we covered the installation process of Outlook, including system requirements and step-by-step instructions for setting up a new account. We also discussed the Outlook interface, highlighting key components such as the Ribbon, Navigation Pane, and Reading Pane.

Key Takeaways:

- Installation Process: Ensure your system meets the requirements and follow the installation steps for a smooth setup.

- Account Creation: Whether for personal or business use, setting up an Outlook account is straightforward.

- Interface Navigation: Familiarize yourself with the Outlook interface to efficiently manage emails and other features.

Chapter 3: Managing Emails

Managing emails is a core function of Outlook. We explored how to compose, send, receive, and read emails. Additionally, we delved into organizing emails using folders, categories, and flags.

Key Takeaways:

- Composing Emails: Learn how to create and format emails, and add attachments to your messages.

- Reading Emails: Use the Inbox and Reading Pane to efficiently read and manage incoming emails.

- Organizing Emails: Utilize folders, categories, and flags to keep your inbox organized and prioritize important messages.

Chapter 4: Working with Contacts

Contacts management is another crucial aspect of Outlook. This chapter explained how to create and manage individual contacts and contact groups. We also covered importing and exporting contacts for seamless data transfer.

Key Takeaways:

- Creating Contacts: Add new contacts with detailed information to your address book.

- Managing Contacts: Edit and update contact information to keep your address book current.

- Contact Groups: Use contact groups to simplify communication with multiple recipients.

- Import/Export Contacts: Easily transfer contact information between Outlook and other platforms.

Chapter 5: Calendar and Scheduling

Outlook's calendar feature is a powerful tool for scheduling and managing appointments and meetings. We discussed creating appointments, setting up recurring events, and using reminders to stay on top of your schedule.

Key Takeaways:

- Calendar Views: Customize your calendar view to suit your preferences.

- Appointments and Meetings: Schedule appointments and send meeting requests with ease.

- Reminders: Set reminders for important events to ensure you never miss a meeting or deadline.

Chapter 6: Tasks and To-Do Lists

Managing tasks and to-do lists in Outlook helps you stay organized and productive. We covered creating and managing tasks, categorizing and prioritizing them, and using the To-Do List feature to track your progress.

Key Takeaways:

- Creating Tasks: Add tasks with detailed descriptions and due dates.

- Organizing Tasks: Categorize and prioritize tasks to manage your workload effectively.

- To-Do List: Use the To-Do List to keep track of your tasks and monitor your progress.

Chapter 7: Notes and Journal

Outlook's Notes and Journal features allow you to keep track of important information and activities. We explored how to create, organize, and manage notes, as well as how to use the Journal to record interactions and tasks.

Key Takeaways:

- Using Notes: Create and organize notes to capture important information quickly.

- Journal Entries: Record interactions and tasks using the Journal for a detailed activity log.

Chapter 8: Outlook Customization

Customizing Outlook allows you to tailor the application to your specific needs. We discussed customizing the Ribbon, Navigation Pane, and applying themes to enhance your user experience.

Key Takeaways:

- Customizing the Ribbon: Add or remove commands and create custom tabs for quick access to frequently used features.

- Navigation Pane: Adjust the size and add shortcuts for easy navigation.

- Outlook Themes: Apply and customize themes to personalize the look and feel of Outlook.

Chapter 9: Advanced Email Management

For advanced users, Outlook offers powerful email management tools. We explored using rules to automate email management, searching and filtering emails, and archiving old messages.

Key Takeaways:

- Email Rules: Create rules to automatically manage incoming emails based on specific criteria.

- Search and Filters: Use advanced search and filters to quickly find emails.

- Email Archiving: Archive old emails to keep your inbox clean and maintain performance.

Chapter 10: Security and Privacy

Maintaining security and privacy in Outlook is crucial. We covered managing junk email, using encryption, and protecting your account with strong passwords and two-factor authentication.

Key Takeaways:

- Junk Email Management: Block unwanted senders and manage your safe senders list.

- Encryption: Encrypt sensitive emails to protect your information.

- Account Security: Use strong passwords and enable two-factor authentication for enhanced security.

Chapter 11: Troubleshooting and Support

Finally, we discussed common issues and solutions in Outlook, along with resources for getting help and support.

Key Takeaways:

- Common Issues: Identify and resolve common problems such as email sending/receiving issues and calendar sync problems.

- Getting Support: Use Outlook's help feature and contact support for additional assistance.

Recap and Final Thoughts

Through this guide, we have provided you with step-by-step instructions to master the basic and advanced features of Outlook. By understanding and applying these key points, you can efficiently manage your emails, contacts, calendar, tasks, and more, ensuring you make the most out of this powerful tool.

Remember, practice is essential. The more you use Outlook and explore its features, the more proficient you will become. Don't hesitate to revisit chapters or sections of this book if you need a refresher on specific topics. With time and experience, you'll find that Outlook can significantly enhance your productivity and organization.

12.2 Final Tips for Outlook Users

As you conclude your journey through this guide on using Outlook, here are some final tips to help you become an even more proficient and efficient user. These tips are designed to enhance your overall experience, improve your productivity, and ensure you make the most of Outlook's capabilities.

1. Stay Organized with Folders and Categories

Creating Folders: One of the simplest ways to keep your inbox organized is by creating folders. Use folders to categorize your emails based on projects, clients, or other relevant criteria. To create a folder, right-click on your Inbox or any existing folder, select "New Folder," and name it appropriately.

Using Categories: Categories are another powerful tool for organizing your emails, tasks, and calendar events. You can assign different colors and names to categories and apply them to items across Outlook. This visual aid helps you quickly identify and prioritize your items. To create or manage categories, go to the Home tab, click on "Categorize," and select "All Categories."

Archiving Old Emails: To prevent your inbox from becoming cluttered, regularly archive old emails that you no longer need immediate access to but want to keep for future reference. You can set up automatic archiving by going to File > Options > Advanced > AutoArchive Settings.

2. Mastering the Search Function

Using Keywords and Filters: Outlook's search function is robust and can save you a lot of time. Use specific keywords, sender names, or dates to find emails quickly. You can also use filters to narrow down your search results by clicking on the search bar and selecting the desired filters such as "From," "Subject," "Has Attachments," and more.

Saving Search Queries: If you frequently search for the same types of emails, consider saving your search queries. After performing a search, click on "Save Search" in the search toolbar. This creates a virtual folder that updates automatically as new emails match your search criteria.

Advanced Search: For more complex searches, use the Advanced Find feature. Press Ctrl + Shift + F to open the Advanced Find window, where you can specify multiple criteria across different fields.

3. Enhancing Email Security

Recognizing Phishing Attempts: Be vigilant about phishing attempts. Look out for suspicious emails that ask for personal information or contain links to unknown websites. Verify the sender's email address and be cautious of emails with urgent or threatening language.

Using Encryption: For sensitive information, use email encryption to protect your messages. To encrypt an email, go to Options > Encrypt > Encrypt with S/MIME. Ensure that both you and the recipient have the necessary certificates installed.

Two-Factor Authentication: Enable two-factor authentication (2FA) for an added layer of security. This requires you to verify your identity using a secondary method, such as a text message or an authentication app, in addition to your password.

4. Optimizing Calendar Management

Setting Up Recurring Events: For regular meetings or events, set up recurring events to save time and ensure consistency. When creating an event, click on "Recurrence" and specify the frequency, such as daily, weekly, or monthly.

Using Time Zones: If you work with people in different time zones, use Outlook's time zone feature to schedule meetings at appropriate times. When creating a new event, click on "Time Zones" in the toolbar and set the start and end times for each time zone.

Sharing Calendars: Share your calendar with colleagues to improve collaboration and transparency. Right-click on your calendar, select "Share," and choose the people you want to share with. You can also specify the level of access they have, such as viewing only or editing permissions.

5. Improving Email Writing

Using Templates: Save time by creating templates for emails that you send frequently. Compose an email, then go to File > Save As > Outlook Template. To use a template, go to Home > New Items > More Items > Choose Form > User Templates in File System.

Personalizing Emails: Personalize your emails by using the recipient's name and referencing previous interactions or relevant information. This makes your emails more engaging and shows that you value the recipient.

Clear and Concise Writing: Keep your emails clear and concise. Use bullet points or numbered lists for easy readability, and ensure your main message is at the beginning of the email. Avoid long paragraphs and unnecessary jargon.

6. Maximizing Task Management

Prioritizing Tasks: Use Outlook's task prioritization features to focus on what's most important. When creating a task, set the priority to High, Normal, or Low. You can also use categories and flags to visually prioritize tasks.

Setting Reminders: Set reminders for your tasks to ensure you stay on track. When creating or editing a task, set a reminder by specifying the date and time. You'll receive a notification when it's time to start or complete the task.

Using the To-Do Bar: The To-Do Bar in Outlook provides a quick overview of your upcoming tasks, calendar events, and flagged emails. To enable the To-Do Bar, go to View > To-Do Bar and select Calendar, Tasks, or both.

7. Integrating Outlook with Other Tools

Syncing with Mobile Devices: Sync Outlook with your mobile devices to stay connected on the go. Download the Outlook app from your device's app store and sign in with your Outlook account. Ensure your email, calendar, and contacts are synced for seamless access.

Connecting with Other Apps: Integrate Outlook with other productivity apps you use, such as Microsoft Teams, OneNote, or third-party tools like Trello or Asana. These integrations can streamline your workflow and improve collaboration.

Using Outlook Add-Ins: Explore Outlook add-ins to enhance your productivity. Go to Home > Get Add-Ins to browse and install add-ins that integrate with services like Zoom, Salesforce, and more.

8. Maintaining Your Outlook Performance

Cleaning Up Your Mailbox: Regularly clean up your mailbox to ensure optimal performance. Use the "Clean Up" tool to remove redundant messages in a conversation. Go to Home > Clean Up and choose the desired option.

Managing Storage: Monitor your mailbox size and manage storage by archiving old emails, emptying the Deleted Items folder, and removing large attachments. Go to File > Tools > Mailbox Cleanup to access various storage management options.

Updating Outlook: Keep your Outlook software up to date to benefit from the latest features and security updates. Enable automatic updates by going to File > Office Account > Update Options and selecting "Enable Updates."

9. Learning and Support Resources

Official Microsoft Resources: Utilize Microsoft's official resources, including the Outlook Help Center, training videos, and user guides. Visit the Microsoft Support website for comprehensive tutorials and troubleshooting tips.

Online Communities: Join online communities and forums where Outlook users share tips, ask questions, and provide solutions. Websites like Reddit, Stack Exchange, and Microsoft Tech Community are valuable resources for peer support.

Continuous Learning: Stay informed about new features and best practices by subscribing to newsletters, following relevant blogs, and attending webinars or training sessions. Continuous learning ensures you remain proficient and up-to-date with Outlook's capabilities.

10. Final Words

Outlook is a powerful tool that, when used effectively, can significantly enhance your productivity and communication. By implementing these tips and continually exploring Outlook's features, you'll become a more efficient and confident user. Remember, the key to mastering Outlook is practice and experimentation. Don't hesitate to try new features, customize your settings, and seek out additional resources to further your knowledge. Happy emailing!

Acknowledgements

*Thank you for purchasing **"Outlook for Beginners: Step-by-Step Instructions".** Your support and interest in enhancing your skills with Outlook are greatly appreciated. Writing this book has been a labor of love, and it is readers like you who make all the effort worthwhile.*

I hope this guide serves as a valuable resource on your journey to mastering Outlook. Whether you are new to the program or looking to brush up on your skills, my goal has been to provide clear, concise, and practical instructions to help you become proficient and confident in using Outlook.

Your feedback is invaluable to me, and I encourage you to share your thoughts and suggestions. If you find this book helpful, please consider leaving a review to help others discover it. Your insights will contribute to future editions and help improve the learning experience for all readers.

Once again, thank you for your support. Wishing you success and productivity in your use of Outlook!

www.ingramcontent.com/pod-product-compliance
Lightning Source LLC
LaVergne TN
LVHW081337050326
832903LV00024B/1185